SCOTTISH
GHOST STORIES

BY

ELLIOTT O'DONNELL

ELLIOTT O'DONNELL

AUTHOR OF

"SOME HAUNTED HOUSES OF ENGLAND AND WALES"

"HAUNTED HOUSES OF LONDON" "GHOSTLY PHENOMENA"

"TRUE GHOST STORIES" "DREAMS AND THEIR MEANINGS"

CONTENTS

CASE

I. THE DEATH BOGLE OF THE CROSS ROADS, AND THE INEXTINGUISHABLE CANDLE OF THE OLD WHITE HOUSE, PITLOCHRY

II. THE TOP ATTIC IN PRINGLE'S MANSION, EDINBURGH

III. THE BOUNDING FIGURE OF "---- HOUSE," NEAR BUCKINGHAM TERRACE, EDINBURGH

IV. JANE OF GEORGE STREET, EDINBURGH

V. THE SALLOW-FACED WOMAN OF NO. -- FORREST ROAD, EDINBURGH

VI. THE PHANTOM REGIMENT OF KILLIECRANKIE

VII. "PEARLIN' JEAN" OF ALLANBANK

VIII. THE DRUMMER OF CORTACHY

IX. THE ROOM BEYOND. AN ACCOUNT OF THE HAUNTINGS OF HENNERSLEY, NEAR AYR

X. "---- HOUSE," NEAR BLYTHSWOOD SQUARE, GLASGOW. THE HAUNTED BATH

XI. THE CHOKING GHOST OF "---- HOUSE," NEAR SANDYFORD PLACE, GLASGOW

XII. THE GREY PIPER AND THE HEAVY COACH OF DONALDGOWERIE HOUSE, PERTH

XIII. THE FLOATING HEAD OF THE BENRACHETT INN, NEAR THE PERTH ROAD, DUNDEE

XIV. THE HAUNTINGS OF "---- HOUSE," IN THE NEIGHBOURHOOD OF THE GREAT WESTERN ROAD, ABERDEEN

XV. THE WHITE LADY OF ROWNAM AVENUE, NEAR STIRLING

XVI. THE GHOST OF THE HINDOO CHILD, OR THE HAUNTINGS OF THE WHITE DOVE HOTEL, NEAR ST. SWITHIN'S STREET, ABERDEEN

XVII. GLAMIS CASTLE

THE DEATH BOGLE OF THE CROSS ROADS, AND THE

INEXTINGUISHABLE CANDLE OF THE OLD WHITE

HOUSE, PITLOCHRY

Several years ago, bent on revisiting Perthshire, a locality which had great attractions for me as a boy, I answered an advertisement in a popular ladies' weekly. As far as I can recollect, it was somewhat to this effect: "Comfortable home offered to a gentleman (a bachelor) at moderate terms in an elderly Highland lady's house at Pitlochry. Must be a strict teetotaller and non-smoker. F.M., Box so-and-so."

The naïveté and originality of the advertisement pleased me. The idea of obtaining as a boarder a young man combining such virtues as abstinence from alcohol and tobacco amused me vastly. And then a bachelor, too! Did she mean to make love to him herself? The sly old thing! She took care to insert the epithet "elderly," in order to avoid suspicion; and there was no doubt about it--she thirsted for matrimony. Being "tabooed" by all the men who had even as much as caught a passing glimpse of her, this was her last resource--she would entrap some unwary stranger, a man with money of course, and inveigle him into marrying her. And there rose up before me visions of a tall, angular, forty-year-old Scottish spinster, with high cheek-bones, virulent, sandy hair, and brawny arms--the sort of woman that ought not to have been a woman at all--the sort that sets all my teeth on edge. Yet it was Pitlochry, heavenly Pitlochry, and there was no one else advertising in that town. That I should suit her in every respect but the matrimonial, I did not doubt. I can pass muster in any company as a teetotaller; I abominate tobacco (leastways it abominates me, which amounts to much about the same thing), and I am, or rather I can be, tolerably amenable, if my surroundings are not positively infernal, and there are no County Council children within shooting distance.

But for once my instincts were all wrong. The advertiser--a Miss Flora Macdonald of "Donald Murray House"--did _not_ resemble my preconception of her in any respect. She was of medium height, and dainty build--a fairy-like creature clad in rustling silks, with wavy, white hair, bright, blue eyes, straight, delicate features, and hands, the shape and slenderness of which at once pronounced her a psychic. She greeted me with all the stately courtesy of the Old School; my portmanteau was taken upstairs by a solemn-eyed lad in the Macdonald tartan; and the tea bell rang me down to a most appetising repast of strawberries and cream, scones, and delicious buttered toast. I fell in love with my

6

hostess--it would be sheer sacrilege to designate such a divine creature by the vulgar term of "landlady"--at once. When one's impressions of a place are at first exalted, they are often, later on, apt to become equally abased. In this case, however, it was otherwise. My appreciation both of Miss Flora Macdonald and of her house daily increased. The food was all that could be desired, and my bedroom, sweet with the perfume of jasmine and roses, presented such a picture of dainty cleanliness, as awakened in me feelings of shame, that it should be defiled by all my dusty, travel-worn accoutrements. I flatter myself that Miss Macdonald liked me also. That she did not regard me altogether as one of the common herd was doubtless, in some degree, due to the fact that she was a Jacobite; and in a discussion on the associations of her romantic namesake, "Flora Macdonald," with Perthshire, it leaked out that our respective ancestors had commanded battalions in Louis XIV.'s far-famed Scottish and Irish Brigades. That discovery bridged gulfs. We were no longer payer and paid--we were friends--friends for life.

A lump comes into my throat as I pen these words, for it is only a short time since I heard of her death.

A week or so after I had settled in her home, I took, at her suggestion, a rest (and, I quite agree with her, it was a very necessary rest) from my writing, and spent the day on Loch Tay, leaving again for "Donald Murray House" at seven o'clock in the evening. It was a brilliant, moonlight night. Not a cloud in the sky, and the landscape stood out almost as clearly as in the daytime. I cycled, and after a hard but thoroughly enjoyable spell of pedalling, eventually came to a standstill on the high road, a mile or two from the first lights of Pitlochry. I halted, not through fatigue, for I was almost as fresh as when I started, but because I was entranced with the delightful atmosphere, and wanted to draw in a few really deep draughts of it before turning into bed. My halting-place was on a triangular plot of grass at the junction of four roads. I propped my machine against a hedge, and stood with my back leaning against a sign-post, and my face in the direction whence I had come. I remained in this attitude for some minutes, probably ten, and was about to remount my bicycle, when I suddenly became icy cold, and a frightful, hideous terror seized and gripped me so hard, that the machine, slipping from my palsied hands, fell to the ground with a crash. The next instant something--for the life of me I knew not what, its outline was so blurred and indefinite-- alighted on the open space in front of me with a soft thud, and remained standing as bolt upright as a cylindrical pillar. From afar off, there then came the low rumble of wheels, which momentarily grew in intensity, until there thundered into view a waggon, weighed down beneath a monstrous stack of hay, on the top of which sat a man in a wide-brimmed straw hat, engaged in a deep confabulation with a boy in corduroys who sprawled beside him. The horse, catching sight of the motionless "thing" opposite me, at once stood still and snorted violently. The man cried out, "Hey! hey! What's the matter with ye, beast?" And then in an hysterical kind of screech, "Great God! What's yon figure that I see? What's yon figure, Tammas?"

The boy immediately raised himself into a kneeling position, and, clutching hold of the man's arm, screamed, "I dinna ken, I dinna ken, Matthew; but take heed, mon, it does na touch me. It's me it's come after, na ye."

The moonlight was so strong that the faces of the speakers were revealed to me with extraordinary vividness, and their horrified expressions were even more startling than was the silent, ghastly figure of the Unknown. The scene comes back to me, here, in my little room in Norwood, with its every detail as clearly marked as on the night it was first enacted. The long range of cone-shaped mountains, darkly silhouetted against the silvery sky, and seemingly hushed in gaping expectancy; the shining, scaly surface of some far-off tarn or river, perceptible only at intervals, owing to the thick clusters of gently nodding pines; the white-washed walls of cottages, glistening amid the dark green denseness of the thickly leaved box trees, and the light, feathery foliage of the golden laburnum; the undulating meadows, besprinkled with gorse and grotesquely moulded crags of granite; the white, the dazzling white roads, saturated with moonbeams; all--all were overwhelmed with stillness--the stillness that belongs, and belongs only, to the mountains, and trees, and plains--the stillness of shadowland. I even counted the buttons, the horn buttons, on the rustics' coats--one was missing from the man's, two from the boy's; and I even noted the sweat-stains under the armpits of Matthew's shirt, and the dents and tears in Tammas's soft wideawake. I observed all these trivialities and more besides. I saw the abrupt rising and falling of the man's chest as his breath came in sharp jerks; the stream of dirty saliva that oozed from between his blackberry-stained lips and dribbled down his chin; I saw their hands--the man's, square-fingered, black-nailed, big-veined, shining with perspiration and clutching grimly at the reins; the boy's, smaller, and if anything rather more grimy--the one pressed flat down on the hay, the other extended in front of him, the palm stretched outwards and all the fingers widely apart.

And while these minute particulars were being driven into my soul, the cause of it all--the indefinable, esoteric column--stood silent and motionless over-against the hedge, a baleful glow emanating from it.

The horse suddenly broke the spell. Dashing its head forward, it broke off at a gallop, and, tearing frantically past the phantasm, went helter-skelter down the road to my left. I then saw Tammas turning a somersault, miraculously saved from falling head first on to the road, by rebounding from the pitchfork which had been wedged upright in the hay, whilst the figure, which followed in their wake with prodigious bounds, was apparently trying to get at him with its spidery arms. But whether it succeeded or not I cannot say, for I was so uncontrollably fearful lest it should return to me, that I mounted my bicycle and rode as I had never ridden before and have never ridden since.

I described the incident to Miss Macdonald on my return. She looked very serious.

"It was stupid of me not to have warned you," she said. "That that particular spot in the road has always--at least ever since I can remember--borne the reputation of being haunted. None of the peasants round here will venture within a mile of it after twilight, so the carters you saw must have been strangers. No one has ever seen the ghost except in the misty form in which it appeared to you. It does not frequent the place every night; it only appears periodically; and its method never varies. It leaps over a wall or hedge, remains stationary till some one approaches, and then pursues them with monstrous springs. The person it touches invariably dies within a year. I well recollect when I was in my teens, on just such a night as this, driving home with my father from Lady Colin Ferner's croquet party at Blair Atholl. When we got to the spot you name, the horse shied, and before I could realise what had happened, we were racing home at a terrific pace. My father and I sat in front, and the groom, a Highland boy from the valley of Ben-y-gloe, behind. Never having seen my father frightened, his agitation now alarmed me horribly, and the more so as my instinct told me it was caused by something other than the mere bolting of the horse. I was soon enlightened. A gigantic figure, with leaps and bounds, suddenly overtook us, and, thrusting out its long, thin arms, touched my father lightly on the hand, and then with a harsh cry, more like that of some strange animal than that of a human being, disappeared. Neither of us spoke till we reached home,--I did not live here then, but in a house on the other side of Pitlochry,--when my father, who was still as white as a sheet, took me aside and whispered, 'Whatever you do, Flora, don't breathe a word of what has happened to your mother, and never let her go along that road at night. It was the death bogle. I shall die within twelve months.' And he did."

Miss Macdonald paused. A brief silence ensued, and she then went on with all her customary briskness: "I cannot describe the thing any more than you can, except that it gave me the impression it had no eyes. But what it was, whether the ghost of a man, woman, or some peculiar beast, I could not, for the life of me, tell. Now, Mr. O'Donnell, have you had enough horrors for one evening, or would you like to hear just one more?"

Knowing that sleep was utterly out of the question, and that one or two more thrills would make very little difference to my already shattered nerves, I replied that I would listen eagerly to anything she could tell me, however horrible. My permission thus gained--and gained so readily--Miss Macdonald, not without, I noticed, one or two apprehensive glances at the slightly rustling curtains, began her narrative, which ran, as nearly as I can remember, as follows:--

"After my father's death, I told my mother about our adventure the night we drove home from Lady Colin Ferner's party, and asked her if she remembered ever having heard anything that could possibly account for the phenomenon. After a few moments' reflection, this is the story she told me:--

THE INEXTINGUISHABLE CANDLE OF THE OLD WHITE HOUSE

There was once a house, known as "The Old White House," that used to stand by the side of the road, close to where you say the horse first took fright. Some people of the name of Holkitt, relations of dear old Sir Arthur Holkitt, and great friends of ours, used to live there. The house, it was popularly believed, had been built on the site of an ancient burial-ground. Every one used to say it was haunted, and the Holkitts had great trouble in getting servants. The appearance of the haunted house did not belie its reputation, for its grey walls, sombre garden, gloomy hall, dark passages and staircase, and sinister-looking attics could not have been more thoroughly suggestive of all kinds of ghostly phenomena. Moreover, the whole atmosphere of the place, no matter how hot and bright the sun, was cold and dreary, and it was a constant source of wonder to every one how Lady Holkitt could live there. She was, however, always cheerful, and used to tell me that nothing would induce her to leave a spot dear to so many generations of her family, and associated with the happiest recollections in her life. She was very fond of company, and there was scarcely a week in the year in which she had not some one staying with her. I can only remember her as widow, her husband, a major in the Gordon Highlanders, having died in India before I was born. She had two daughters, Margaret and Alice, both considered very handsome, but some years older than I. This difference in age, however, did not prevent our being on very friendly terms, and I was constantly invited to their house--in the summer to croquet and archery, in the winter to balls. Like most elderly ladies of that period, Lady Holkitt was very fond of cards, and she and my mother used frequently to play bezique and cribbage, whilst the girls and I indulged in something rather more frivolous. On those occasions the carriage always came for us at ten, since my mother, for some reason or other--I had a shrewd suspicion it was on account of the alleged haunting--would never return home after that time. When she accepted an invitation to a ball, it was always conditionally that Lady Holkitt would put us both up for the night, and the carriage used, then, to come for us the following day, after one o'clock luncheon. I shall never forget the last time I went to a dance at "The Old White House," though it is now rather more than fifty years ago. My mother had not been very well for some weeks, having, so she thought, taken cold internally. She had not had a doctor, partly because she did not feel ill enough, and partly because the only medical man near us was an apothecary, of whose skill she had a very poor opinion. My mother had quite made up her mind to accompany me to the ball, but at the last moment, the weather being appalling, she yielded to advice, and my aunt Norah, who happened to be staying with us at the time, chaperoned me instead. It was snowing when we set out, and as it snowed all through the night and most of the next day, the roads were completely blocked, and we had to remain at "The Old White House" from Monday evening till the following Thursday. Aunt Norah and I occupied separate bedrooms, and mine was at the end of a long passage away from everybody else's. Prior to this my mother and I had always shared a room--the only really pleasant one, so I thought, in the house--overlooking the front lawn. But on this occasion there being a number of visitors, belated like ourselves, we had to squeeze in wherever we could; and as my aunt and I were to have separate rooms (my aunt liking a room to herself), it was natural that she should be allotted the largest and most comfortable. Consequently, she was domiciled in the wing where all the other visitors slept, whilst I was forced to retreat to a passage on the other side of the house, where, with the exception of my apartment, there were none other but lumber-rooms. All went smoothly and happily, and nothing interrupted the harmony of our visit, till the night before we returned home. We had had supper--our meals were differently arranged in those days--and Margaret and I were ascending the staircase on our way to bed, when Alice, who had run upstairs ahead of us, met us with a scared face.

"Oh, do come to my room!" she cried. "Something has happened to Mary." (Mary was one of the housemaids.)

We both accompanied her, and, on entering her room, found Mary seated on a chair, sobbing hysterically. One only had to glance at the girl to see that she was suffering from some very severe shock. Though normally red-cheeked and placid, in short, a very healthy, stolid creature, and the last person to be easily perturbed, she was now without a vestige of colour, whilst the pupils of her eyes were dilated with terror, and her entire body, from the crown of her head to the soles of her feet, shook as if with ague. I was immeasurably shocked to see her.

"Why, Mary," Margaret exclaimed, "whatever is the matter? What has happened?"

"It's the candle, miss," the girl gasped, "the candle in Miss Trevor's room. I can't put it out."

"You can't put it out, why, what nonsense!" Margaret said. "Are you mad?"

"It is as true as I sit here, miss," Mary panted. "I put the candle on the mantelpiece while I set the room to rights, and when I had finished and came to blow it out, I couldn't. I blew, and blew, and blew, but it hadn't any effect, and then I grew afraid, miss, horribly afraid," and here she buried her face in her hands, and shuddered. "I've never been frightened like this before, miss," she returned slowly, "and I've come away and left the candle burning."

"How absurd of you," Margaret scolded. "We must go and put it out at once. I have a good mind to make you come with us, Mary--but there! Stay where you are, and for goodness' sake stop crying, or everyone in the house will hear you."

So saying, Margaret hurried off,--Alice and I accompanying her,--and on arriving outside my room, the door of which was wide open, we perceived the lighted candle standing in the position Mary had described. I looked at the girls, and perceived, in spite of my endeavours not to perceive it, the unmistakable signs of a great fear--fear of something they suspected but dared not name--lurking in the corners of their eyes.

"Who will go first?" Margaret demanded. No one spoke.

"Well then," she continued, "I will," and, suiting the action to the word, she stepped over the threshold. The moment she did so, the door began to close. "This is curious!" she cried. "Push!"

We did; we all three pushed; but, despite our efforts, the door came resolutely to, and we were shut out. Then before we had time to recover from our astonishment, it flew open; but before we could cross the threshold, it came violently to in the same manner as before. Some unseen force held it against us.

"Let us make one more effort," Margaret said, "and if we don't succeed, we will call for help."

Obeying her instructions, we once again pushed. I was nearest the handle, and in some manner,--how, none of us could ever explain,--just as the door opened of its own accord, I slipped and fell inside. The door then closed immediately with a bang, and, to my unmitigated horror, I found myself alone in the room. For some seconds I was spellbound, and could not even collect my thoughts sufficiently to frame a reply to the piteous entreaties of the Holkitts, who kept banging on the door, and imploring me to tell them what was happening. Never in the hideous excitement of nightmare had I experienced such a terror as the terror that room conveyed to my mind. Though nothing was to be seen, nothing but the candle, the light of which was peculiarly white and vibrating, I felt the presence of something inexpressibly menacing and horrible. It was in the light, the atmosphere, the furniture, everywhere. On all sides it surrounded me, on all sides I was threatened--threatened in a manner that was strange and deadly. Something suggesting to me that the source of evil originated in the candle, and that if I could succeed in extinguishing the light I should free myself from the ghostly presence, I advanced towards the mantelpiece, and, drawing in a deep breath, blew--blew with the energy born of desperation. It had no effect. I repeated my efforts; I blew frantically, madly, but all to no purpose; the candle still burned--burned softly and mockingly. Then a fearful terror seized me, and, flying to the opposite side of the room, I buried my face against the wall, and waited for what the sickly beatings of my heart warned me was coming. Constrained to look, I slightly, only very, very slightly, moved round, and there, there, floating stealthily towards me through the air, came the candle, the vibrating, glowing, baleful candle. I hid my face again, and prayed God to let me faint. Nearer and nearer drew the light; wilder and wilder the wrenches at the door. Closer and closer I pressed myself to the wall. And then, then when the final throes of agony were more than human heart and brain could stand, there came the suspicion, the suggestion of a touch--of a touch so horrid that my prayers were at last answered, and I fainted. When I recovered, I was in Margaret's room, and half a dozen well-known forms were gathered round me. It appears that with the collapse of my body on the floor, the door, that had so effectually resisted every effort to turn the handle, immediately flew open, and I was discovered lying on the ground with the candle--still alight--on the ground beside me. My aunt experienced no difficulty in blowing out the refractory candle, and I was carried with the greatest tenderness into the other wing of the house, where I slept that night. Little was said about the incident next day, but all who knew of it expressed in their faces the utmost anxiety--an anxiety which, now that I had recovered, greatly puzzled me. On our return home, another shock awaited me; we found to our dismay that my mother was seriously ill, and that the doctor, who had been sent for from Perth the previous evening, just about the time of my adventure with the candle, had stated that she might not survive the day. His warning was fulfilled--she died at sunset. Her death, of course, may have had nothing at all to do with the candle episode, yet it struck me then as an odd coincidence, and seems all the more strange to me after hearing your account of the bogle that touched your dear father in the road, so near the spot where the Holkitts' house once stood. I could never discover whether Lady Holkitt or her daughters ever saw anything of a superphysical nature in their house; after my experience they were always very reticent on that subject, and naturally I did not like to press it. On Lady Holkitt's death, Margaret and Alice sold the house, which was eventually pulled down, as no one would live in it, and I believe the ground on which it stood is now a turnip field. That, my dear, is all I can tell you.

* * * * *

"Now, Mr. O'Donnell," Miss Macdonald added, "having heard our experiences, my mother's and mine, what is your opinion? Do you think the phenomenon of the candle was in any way connected with the bogle both you and I have seen, or are the hauntings of 'The Old White House' entirely separate from those of the road?"

CASE II

THE TOP ATTIC IN PRINGLE'S MANSION, EDINBURGH

A charming lady, Miss South, informs me that no house interested her more, as a child, than Pringle's Mansion, Edinburgh. Pringle's Mansion, by the bye, is not the real name of the house, nor is the original building still standing--the fact is, my friend has been obliged to disguise the locality for fear of an action for slander of title, such as happened in the Egham Case of 1904-7.

Miss South never saw--save in a picture--the house that so fascinated her; but through repeatedly hearing about it from her old nurse, she felt that she knew it by heart, and used to amuse herself hour after hour in the nursery, drawing diagrams of the rooms and passages, which, to make quite realistic, she named and numbered.

There was the Admiral's room, Madame's room, Miss Ophelia's room, Master Gregory's room, Letty's (the nurse's) room, the cook's room, the butler's room, the housemaid's room--and--the Haunted Room.

The house was very old--probably the sixteenth century--and was concealed from the thoroughfare by

21

a high wall that enclosed it on all sides. It had no garden, only a large yard, covered with faded yellow paving-stones, and containing a well with an old-fashioned roller and bucket.

When the well was cleaned out, an event which took place periodically on a certain date, every utensil in the house was called into requisition for ladling out the water, and the Admiral, himself supervising, made every servant in the establishment take an active part in the proceedings. On one of these occasions, the Admiral announced his intention of going down the well in the bucket. That was a rare moment in Letty's life, for when the Admiral had been let down in the bucket, the rope broke!

Indeed, the thought of what the Laird would say when he came up, almost resulted in his not coming up at all. However, some one, rather bolder than the rest, retained sufficient presence of mind to effect a rescue, and the timid ones, thankful enough to survive the explosion, had to be content on "half-rations till further orders."

But in spite of its association with such a martinet, and in spite of her ghostly experiences in it, Letty loved the house, and was never tired of singing its praises.

It was a two-storeyed mansion, with roomy cellars but no basement. There were four reception-rooms--all oak-panelled--on the ground floor; numerous kitchen offices, including a cosy housekeeper's room; and a capacious entrance hall, in the centre of which stood a broad oak staircase. The cellars, three in number, and chiefly used as lumber-rooms, were deep down and dank and horrid.

On the first floor eight bedrooms opened on to a gallery overlooking the hall, and the top storey, where the servants slept, consisted solely of attics connected with one another by dark, narrow passages. It was one of these attics that was haunted, although, as a matter of fact, the ghost had been seen in all parts of the house.

When Letty entered the Admiral's service she was but a bairn, and had never even heard of ghosts; nor did the other servants apprise her of the hauntings, having received strict injunctions not to do so from the Laird.

But Letty's home, humble though it was, had been very bright and cheerful, and the dark precincts of the mansion filled her with dismay. Without exactly knowing why she was afraid, she shrank in terror from descending into the cellars, and felt anything but pleased at the prospect of sleeping alone in an attic. Still nothing occurred to really alarm her till about a month after her arrival. It was early in the evening, soon after twilight, and she had gone down into one of the cellars to look for a boot-jack, which the Admiral swore by all that was holy must be found before supper. Placing the light she had brought with her on a packing-case, she was groping about among the boxes, when she perceived, to her astonishment, that the flame of the candle had suddenly turned blue. She then felt icy cold, and was much startled on hearing a loud clatter as of some metal instrument on the stone floor in the far-off corner of the cellar. Glancing in the direction of the noise, she saw, looking at her, two eyes--two obliquely set, lurid, light eyes, full of the utmost devilry. Sick with terror and utterly unable to account for what she beheld, she stood stock-still, her limbs refusing to move, her throat parched, her tongue tied. The clanging was repeated, and a shadowy form began slowly to crawl towards her. She dared not afterwards surmise what would have happened to her, had not the Laird himself come down at this moment. At the sound of his stentorian voice the phantasm vanished. But the shock had been too much for Letty; she fainted, and the Admiral, carrying her upstairs as carefully as if she had been his own daughter, gave peremptory orders that she should never again be allowed to go into the cellar alone.

But now that Letty herself had witnessed a manifestation, the other servants no longer felt bound to secrecy, and soon poured into her ears endless accounts of the hauntings.

Every one, they informed her, except Master Gregory and Perkins (the butler) had seen one or other of the ghosts, and the cellar apparition was quite familiar to them all. They also declared that there were other parts of the house quite as badly haunted as the cellar, and it might have been partly owing to these gruesome stories that poor Letty always felt scared, when crossing the passages leading to the attics. As she was hastening down one of them, early one morning, she heard some one running after her. Thinking it was one of the other servants, she turned round, pleased to think that some one else was up early too, and saw to her horror a dreadful-looking object, that seemed to be partly human and partly animal. The body was quite small, and its face bloated, and covered with yellow spots. It had an enormous animal mouth, the lips of which, moving furiously without emitting any sound, showed that the creature was endeavouring to speak but could not. The moment Letty screamed for help the phantasm vanished.

But her worst experience was yet to come. The spare attic which she was told was so badly haunted that no one would sleep in it, was the room next to hers. It was a room Letty could well believe was haunted, for she had never seen another equally gloomy. The ceiling was low and sloping, the window tiny, and the walls exhibited all sorts of odd nooks and crannies. A bed, antique and worm-eaten, stood in one recess, a black oak chest in another, and at right angles with the door, in another recess, stood a wardrobe that used to creak and groan alarmingly every time Letty walked a long the passage. Once she heard a chuckle, a low, diabolical chuckle, which she fancied came from the chest; and once, when the door of the room was open, she caught the glitter of a pair of eyes--the same pale, malevolent eyes that had so frightened her in the cellar. From her earliest childhood Letty had been periodically given to somnambulism, and one night, just about a year after she went into service, she got out of bed, and walked, in her sleep, into the Haunted Room. She awoke to find herself standing, cold and shivering, in the middle of the floor, and it was some seconds before she realised where she was. Her horror, when she did discover where she was, is not easily described. The room was bathed in moonlight, and the beams, falling with noticeable brilliancy on each piece of furniture the room contained, at once riveted Letty's attention, and so fascinated her that she found herself utterly unable to move. A terrible and most unusual silence predominated everywhere, and although Letty's senses were wonderfully and painfully on the alert, she could not catch the slightest sound from any of the rooms on the landing.

The night was absolutely still, no breath of wind, no rustle of leaves, no flapping of ivy against the window; yet the door suddenly swung back on its hinges and slammed furiously. Letty felt that this was the work of some supernatural agency, and, fully expecting that the noise had awakened the cook, who was a light sleeper (or pretended she was), listened in a fever of excitement to hear her get out of bed and call out. The slightest noise and the spell that held her prisoner would, Letty felt sure, be broken. But the same unbroken silence prevailed. A sudden rustling made Letty glance fearfully at the bed; and she perceived, to her terror, the valance swaying violently, to and fro.

Sick with fear, she was now constrained to stare in abject helplessness. Presently there was a slight, very slight movement on the mattress, the white dust cover rose, and, under it, Letty saw the outlines of what she took to be a human figure, gradually take shape. Hoping, praying, that she was mistaken, and that what appeared to be on the bed was but a trick of her imagination, she continued staring in an agony of anticipation. But the figure remained--extended at full length like a corpse. The minutes slowly passed, a church clock boomed two, and the body moved. Letty's jaw fell, her eyes almost bulged from her head, whilst her fingers closed convulsively on the folds of her night-dress. The unmistakable sound of breathing now issued from the region of the bed, and the dust-cover commenced slowly to slip aside. Inch by inch it moved, until first of all Letty saw a few wisps of dark hair, then a few more, then a thick cluster; then something white and shining--a protruding forehead; then dark, very dark brows; then two eyelids, yellow, swollen, and fortunately tightly closed; then--a purple conglomeration of Letty knew not what--of anything but what was human. The sight was so monstrous it appalled her; and she was overcome with a species of awe and repulsion, for which the language of mortality has no sufficiently energetic expression. She momentarily forgot that what she looked on was merely superphysical, but regarded it as something alive, something that ought to have been a child, comely and healthy as herself--and she hated it. It was an outrage on maternity, a blot on nature, a filthy discredit to the house, a blight, a sore, a gangrene. It turned over in its sleep, the cover was hurled aside, and a grotesque object, round, pulpy, webbed, and of leprous whiteness--an object which Letty could hardly associate with a hand--came grovelling out. Letty's stomach heaved; the thing was beastly, indecent, vile, it ought not to live! And the idea of killing flashed through her mind. Boiling over with indignation and absurdly forgetful of her surroundings, she turned round and groped for a stone to smash it. The moonlight on her naked toes brought her to her senses--the thing in the bed was a devil! Though brought up a member of the Free Church, with an abhorrence of anything that could in any way be contorted into Papist practices, Letty crossed herself. As she did so, a noise in the passage outside augmented her terror. She strained her ears painfully, and the sound developed into a footstep, soft, light, and surreptitious. It came gently towards the door; it paused outside, and Letty intuitively felt that it was listening. Her suspense was now so intolerable, that it was almost with a feeling of relief that she beheld the door slowly--very slowly--begin to open. A little wider--a little wider--and yet a little wider; but still nothing came. Ah! Letty's heart turned to ice. Another inch, and a shadowy something slipped through and began to wriggle itself stealthily over the floor. Letty tried to divert her gaze, but could not--an irresistible, magnetic attraction kept her eyes glued to the gradually approaching horror. When within a few feet of her it halted; and again Letty felt it was listening-- listening to the breathing on the bed, which was heavy and bestial. Then it twisted round, and Letty watched

28

it crawl into the wardrobe. After this there was a long and anxious wait. Then Letty saw the wardrobe door slyly open, and the eyes of the cellar--inexpressibly baleful, and glittering like burnished steel in the strong phosphorescent glow of the moon, peep out,-- not at her but _through_ her,--at the object lying on the bed. There were not only eyes, this time, but a form,--vague, misty, and irregular, but still with sufficient shape to enable Letty to identify it as that of a woman, tall and thin, and with a total absence of hair, which was emphasised in the most lurid and ghastly fashion. With a snakelike movement, the evil thing slithered out of the wardrobe, and, gliding past Letty, approached the bed. Letty was obliged to follow every proceeding. She saw the thing deftly snatch the bolster from under the sleeping head; noted the gleam of hellish satisfaction in its eyes as it pressed the bolster down; and watched the murdered creature's contortions grow fainter, and fainter, until they finally ceased. The eyes then left the room; and from afar off, away below, in the abysmal cellars of the house, came the sound of digging--faint, very faint, but unquestionably digging. This terminated the grim, phantasmal drama for that night at least, and Letty, chilled to the bone, but thoroughly alert, escaped to her room. She spent her few remaining hours of rest wide-awake, determining never to go to bed again without fastening one of her arms to the iron staples.

With regard the history of the house, Letty never learned anything more remarkable than that, long ago, an idiot child was supposed to have been murdered in the haunted attic--by whom, tradition did not say. The Admiral and his family left Pringle's Mansion the year Letty became Miss South's nurse, and as no one would stay in the house, presumably on account of the hauntings, it was pulled down, and an inexcusably inartistic edifice was erected in its place.

CASE III

THE BOUNDING FIGURE OF "---- HOUSE," NEAR BUCKINGHAM TERRACE, EDINBURGH

No one is more interested in Psychical Investigation Work than Miss Torfrida Vincent, one of the three beautiful daughters of Mrs. H. de B. Vincent, who is, herself, still in the heyday of life, and one of the loveliest of the society women I have met. Though I have known her sisters several years, I only met Torfrida for the first time a few months ago, when she was superintending the nursing of her mother, who had just undergone an operation for appendicitis. One day, when I was visiting my convalescent friend, Torfrida informed me that she knew of a haunted house in Edinburgh, a case which she felt sure would arouse my interest and enthusiasm. "It is unfortunate," she added somewhat regretfully, "that I cannot tell you the number of the house, but as I have given my word of honour to disclose it to no one, I feel sure you will excuse me. Indeed, my friends the Gordons, who extracted the promise from me, have got into sad trouble with their landlord for leaving the house under the pretext that it was haunted, and he has threatened to prosecute them for slander of title."

The house in question has no claim to antiquity. It may be eighty years old--perhaps a little older--and was, at the time of which I speak, let out in flats. The Gordons occupied the second storey; the one above them was untenanted, and used as a storage place for furniture; the first floor and ground floor were divided into chambers and offices. They had not been in their new quarters more than a week, when Mrs. Gordon asked the night porter who it was that made such a noise, racing up their stairs between two and three in the morning. It had awakened her every night, she told him, and she would be glad if the disturbance were discontinued. "I am sorry, Madam, but I cannot imagine who it can be," the man replied. "Of course, it may be some one next door, sounds are so often deceptive; no one inhabits the rooms above you." But Mrs. Gordon was not at all convinced, and made up her mind to complain to the landlord should it occur again. That night nothing happened, but the night after she was roused from her sleep at two o'clock, by a feeling that something dreadful, some dire catastrophe, was about to take place. The house was very still, and beyond the far-away echoes of a policeman's patrol on the hard pavement outside, nothing, absolutely nothing, broke the universal, and as it seemed to her, unnatural silence. Generally at night-time there are sounds one likes to assure oneself are too trivial to be heard during the day--the creaking of boards, stairs (nearly always stairs), and the tapping of some leaf (of course some leaf) at the windows. Who has not heard such sounds, and who in his heart of hearts has not been only too well aware that they are nocturnal, exclusively nocturnal. The shadows of evening bring with them visitors; prying, curious visitors; grim and ghastly visitors; grey, esoteric visitors; visitors from a world seemingly inconsequent, wholly incomprehensible. Mrs. Gordon did not believe in ghosts. She scoffed at the idea of ghosts, and, like so many would-be wits, unreasonably brave by day, and the reverse by night, had hitherto attributed banshees and the like to cats and other animals. But now,--now when all was dark,--pitch dark and hushed, and she, for aught she knew to the contrary, the only one, in that great rambling building, awake, she reviewed again and again, in her mind, that rushing up the stairs. The wind! It could not have been the wind. The wind shuts doors, and rattles windows, and moans, and sighs, and howls and screeches, but it does not walk the house in boots. Neither do rats! And if she had imagined the noises, why did she not imagine other things; why, for example, did she not see tables dance, and tea-urns walk? All that would be fancy, unblushing, genuine fancy, and if she conjured up one absurdity, why not another! That was a conundrum for any sceptic. Thus did she argue, naturally and logically, in the quite sensible fashion of a lawyer, or a scientist; yet, all the while, her senses told her that the atmosphere of the house had undergone some profoundly subtle and unaccountable change,--a change that brought with it a presence, at once sinister and hostile. She longed to strike a light and awake one of her daughters--Diana, by preference; since Diana was the least likely to mind being disturbed, and had the strongest nerves. She made a start, and, loosening the bedclothes that she always liked tightly tucked round her, thrust out a quivering toe. The next instant she drew it back with a tiny gasp of terror. The cold darkness without had suggested to her mind a great, horny hand, mal-shaped and murderous, that was lying in wait to seize her. A deadly sickness overcame her, and she lay back on the pillow, her heart beating with outrageous irregularity and loudness. Very slowly she recovered, and, holding her breath, sidled to the far edge of the bed, and with a dexterous movement, engendered by the desperation of fear, made a lightning-like dab in the direction of the electric bell. Her soft, pink finger missed the mark, and coming in violent contact with the wall, bent the carefully polished nail. She bit her lips to stop a cry of pain, and shrinking back within the folds of her dainty lace embroidered nightdress, abandoned herself to despair. Her consciousness of the Unknown Presence increased, and she instinctively felt the thing pass through the closed door, down on to the landing outside, when it dashed upstairs with a loud clatter, and, entering the lumber-room immediately overhead, began bounding as if its feet were tied together, backwards and forwards across the floor. After continuing for fully half an hour, the noises abruptly ceased and the house resumed its accustomed quiet. At breakfast, Mrs. Gordon asked her daughters if they had heard anything in the night, and they laughingly said "No, not even a mouse!"

There was now an intermission of the disturbances, and no further demonstration occurred for about a month. Diana was then sleeping in her mother's room, Mrs. Gordon being away on a visit to Lady Voss, who was entertaining a party of friends at her shooting-box in Argyle. One evening, as Diana was going into her bedroom to prepare for dinner, she saw the door suddenly swing open, and something, she could not tell what--it was so blurred and indistinct--come out with a bound. Tearing past her on to the landing, it rushed up the stairs with so much clatter that Diana imagined, though she could see nothing, that it must have on its feet, heavy lumbering boots. Filled with an irresistible curiosity, in spite of her alarm, Diana ran after it, and, on reaching the upper storey, heard it making a terrific racket in the room above the one in which she now slept. Nothing daunted, however, she boldly approached, and, flinging open the door, perceived its filmy outline standing before a shadowy and very antique eight-day clock, which apparently it was in the habit of winding. A great fear now fell on Diana. What was the thing? And supposing it should turn round and face her, what should she see? She was entirely isolated from her sisters, and the servants--alone--the light fading--in a big, gloomy room full of strange old furniture which suggested hiding-places for all sorts of grim possibilities. She was assured now that the thing she had followed was nothing human, neither was it a delusion, for when

she shut her eyes and opened them, it was still there--
and, oddly enough, it was now more distinct than it
was when she had seen it downstairs. A curious
feeling of helplessness stole over Diana; the power of
speech forsook her; and her limbs grew rigid. She was
so fearful, too, of attracting the notice of the
mysterious thing that she hardly dare breathe, and
each pulsation of her heart sent cold chills of
apprehension down her spine. Once she endured
agonies through a mad desire to sneeze, and once her
lips opened to scream as something suspiciously like
the antennæ of a huge beetle, and which she
subsequently discovered was a "devil's coach-horse,"
tickled the calf of her leg. She fancied, too, that all
sorts of queer shapes lurked in the passage behind
her, and that innumerable unseen eyes were
malignantly rejoicing in her terror. At last, the climax
to her suspense seemed at hand. The unknown thing,
until now too busy with the clock to take heed of her,
paused for a moment or so, as if undecided what to do
next, and then slowly began to veer round. But the
faint echo of a voice below, calling her by name, broke
the hypnotic spell that bound Diana to the floor, and
with a frantic spring she cleared the threshold of the
room. She then tore madly downstairs, never halting
till she reached the dining-room, where she sank on a
sofa, and, more dead than alive, panted out to her
amazed sisters a full account of all that had
transpired.

That night she shared her sister's bedroom, but
neither she nor her sister slept.

From this time till the return of Mrs. Gordon, nothing happened. It was one evening after she came back, when she was preparing to get into bed, that the door of her own room unexpectedly opened, and she saw standing, on the threshold, the unmistakable figure of a man, short and broad, with a great width of shoulders, and very long arms. He was clad in a peajacket, blue serge trousers, and jack-boots. He had a big, round, brutal head, covered with a tangled mass of yellow hair, but where his face ought to have been there was only a blotch, underlying which Mrs. Gordon detected the semblance to something fiendishly vindictive and immeasurably nasty. But, in spite of the horror his appearance produced, her curiosity was aroused with regard to the two objects he carried in his hands, one of which looked like a very bizarre bundle of red and white rags, and the other a small bladder of lard. Whilst she was staring at them in dumb awe, he swung round, and, hitching them savagely under his armpits, rushed across the landing, and, with a series of apish bounds, sprang up the staircase and disappeared in the gloom.

This was the climax; Mrs. Gordon felt another such encounter would kill her. So, in spite of the fact that she had taken the flat for a year, and had only just commenced her tenancy, she packed up her goods and left the very next day. The report that the building was haunted spread rapidly, and Mrs. Gordon had many indignant letters from the landlord. She naturally made inquiries as to the early history of the house, but of the many tales she listened to, only one, the authenticity of which she could not guarantee, seemed to suggest any clue to the haunting.

It was said that a retired Captain in the Merchant Service, many years previously, had rented the rooms she had occupied.

He was an extraordinary individual, and, despite the fact that he had lived so far inland, would never wear any but nautical clothes--blue jersey and trousers, reefer coat and jack-boots. But this was not his only peculiarity. His love of grog eventually brought on delirium tremens, and his excessive irritability in the interval between each attack was a source of anxiety to all who came in contact with him. At that time there happened to be a baby in the rooms overhead, whose crying so annoyed the Captain that he savagely informed its mother that if she did not keep it quiet, he would not be answerable for the consequences. His warnings having no effect, he flew upstairs one day, when she was temporarily absent, and, snatching up the bread knife from the table, decapitated the infant. He then stuffed both its head and body into a grandfather's clock which stood in one corner of the room, and, retiring to his own quarters, drank till he was insensible.

He was, of course, arrested on a charge of murder, but being found "insane" he was committed during His Majesty's pleasure to a lunatic asylum.

He eventually committed suicide by opening an artery in his leg with one of his finger-nails.

As the details of this tragedy filled in so well with the phenomena they had witnessed, the Gordons could not help regarding the story as a very probable explanation of the hauntings. But, remember, its authenticity is dubious.

CASE IV

JANE OF GEORGE STREET, EDINBURGH

"The news that, for several years at any rate, George Street, Edinburgh, was haunted," wrote a correspondent of mine some short time ago, "might cause no little surprise to many of its inhabitants." And my friend proceeded to relate his experience of the haunting, which I will reproduce as nearly as possible in his own words. I quote from memory, having foolishly destroyed the letter.

* * * * *

I was walking in a leisurely way along George Street the other day, towards Strunalls, where I get my cigars, and had arrived opposite No. --, when I suddenly noticed, just ahead of me, a tall lady of remarkably graceful figure, clad in a costume which, even to an ignoramus in fashions like myself, seemed extraordinarily out of date. In my untechnical language it consisted of a dark blue coat and skirt, trimmed with black braid. The coat had a very high collar, turned over to show a facing of blue velvet, its sleeves were very full at the shoulders, and a band of blue velvet drew it tightly in at the waist. Moreover, unlike every other lady I saw, she wore a small hat, which I subsequently learned was a toque, with one white and one blue plume placed moderately high at the side. The only other conspicuous items of her dress, the effect of which was, on the whole, quiet, were white glacé gloves,--over which dangled gold curb bracelets with innumerable pendants,--shoes, which were of patent leather with silver buckles and rather high Louis heels, and fine, blue silk openwork stockings. So much for her dress. Now for her herself. She was a strikingly fair woman with very pale yellow hair and a startlingly white complexion; and this latter peculiarity so impressed me that I hastened my steps, determining to get a full view of her. Passing her with rapid strides, I looked back, and as I did so a cold chill ran through me,--what I looked at was--the face of the dead. I slowed down and allowed her to take the lead.

I now observed that, startling as she was, no one else seemed to notice her. One or two people obviously, though probably unconsciously, possessing the germs of psychism, shivered when they passed her, but as they neither slackened their pace nor turned to steal a second look, I concluded they had not seen her. Without glancing either to the right or left, she moved steadily on, past Molton's the confectioner's, past Perrin's the hatter's. Once, I thought she was coming to a halt, and that she intended crossing the road, but no--on, on, on, till we came to D---- Street. There we were preparing to cross over, when an elderly gentleman walked deliberately into her. I half expected to hear him apologise, but naturally nothing of the sort happened; she was only too obviously a phantom, and, in accordance with the nature of a phantom, she passed right through him. A few yards farther on, she came to an abrupt pause, and then, with a slight inclination of her head as if meaning me to follow, she glided into a chemist's shop. She was certainly not more than six feet ahead of me when she passed through the door, and I was even nearer than that to her when she suddenly disappeared as she stood before the counter. I asked the chemist if he could tell me anything about the lady who had just entered his shop, but he merely turned away and laughed.

"Lady!" he said; "what are you talking about? You're a bit out of your reckoning. This isn't the first of April. Come, what do you want?"

I bought a bottle of formamints, and reluctantly and regretfully turned away. That night I dreamed I again saw the ghost. I followed her up George Street just as I had done in reality; but when she came to the chemist's shop, she turned swiftly round. "I'm Jane!" she said in a hollow voice. "Jane! Only Jane!" and with that name ringing in my ears I awoke.

Some days elapsed before I was in George Street again. The weather had in the meanwhile undergone one of those sudden and violent changes, so characteristic of the Scottish climate. The lock-gates of heaven had been opened and the rain was descending in cataracts. The few pedestrians I encountered were enveloped in mackintoshes, and carried huge umbrellas, through which the rain was soaking, and pouring off from every point. Everything was wet--everywhere was mud. The water, splashing upwards, saturated the tops of my boots and converted my trousers into sodden sacks. Some weather isn't fit for dogs, but this weather wasn't good enough for tadpoles--even fish would have kicked at it and kept in their holes. Imagine, then, the anomaly! Amidst all this aqueous inferno, this slippery-sloppery, filth-bespattering inferno, a spotlessly clean apparition in blue without either waterproof or umbrella. I refer to Jane. She suddenly appeared, as I was passing The Ladies' Tea Association Rooms, walking in front of me. She looked just the same as when I last saw her--spick and span, and--dry. I repeat the word--dry--for that is what attracted my attention most. Despite the deluge, not a single raindrop touched her--the plumes on her toque were splendidly erect and curly, her shoe-buckles sparkled, her patent leathers were spotless, whilst the cloth of her coat and skirt looked as sheeny as if they had but just come from Keeley's.

Anxious to get another look at her face, I quickened my pace, and, darting past her, gazed straight into her countenance. The result was a severe shock. The terror of what I saw--the ghastly horror of her dead white face--sent me reeling across the pavement. I let her pass me, and, impelled by a sickly fascination, followed in her wake.

Outside a jeweller's stood a hansom--quite a curiosity in these days of motors--and, as Jane glided past, the horse shied. I have never seen an animal so terrified. We went on, and at the next crossing halted. A policeman had his hand up checking the traffic. His glance fell on Jane--the effect was electrical. His eyes bulged, his cheeks whitened, his chest heaved, his hand dropped, and he would undoubtedly have fallen had not a good Samaritan, in the guise of a non-psychical public-house loafer, held him up. Jane was now close to the chemist's, and it was with a sigh of relief that I saw her glide in and disappear.

Had there been any doubt at all, after my first encounter with Jane, as to her being superphysical, there was certainly none now. The policeman's paroxysm of fear and the horse's fit of shying were facts. What had produced them? I alone knew--and I knew for certain--it was Jane. Both man and animal saw what I saw. Hence the phantom was not subjective; it was not illusionary; it was a _bona fide_

spirit manifestation--a visitant from the other world--
the world of earthbound souls. Jane fascinated me. I
made endless researches in connection with her, and,
in answer to one of my inquiries, I was informed that
eighteen years ago--that is to say, about the time
Jane's dress was in fashion--the chemist's shop had
been occupied by a dressmaker of the name of
Bosworth. I hunted up Miss Bosworth's address and
called on her. She had retired from business and was
living in St. Michael's Road, Bournemouth. I came to
the point straight.

"Can you give me any information," I asked, "about a
lady whose Christian name was Jane?"

"That sounds vague!" Miss Bosworth said. "I've met a
good many Janes in my time."

"But not Janes with pale yellow hair, and white
eyebrows and eyelashes!" And I described her in
detail.

"How do you come to know about her?" Miss
Bosworth said, after a long pause.

"Because," I replied with a certain slowness and
deliberation characteristic of me, "because I've seen
her ghost!"

Of course I knew Miss Bosworth was no sceptic--the
moment my eyes rested on her I saw she was psychic,
and that the superphysical was often at her elbow.

Accordingly, I was not in the least surprised at her look of horror.

"What!" she exclaimed, "is she still there? I thought she would surely be at rest now!"

"Who was she?" I inquired. "Come--you need not be afraid of me. I have come here solely because the occult has always interested me. Who was Jane, and why should her ghost haunt George Street?"

"It happened a good many years ago," Miss Bosworth replied, "in 1892. In answer to an advertisement I saw in one of the daily papers, I called on a Miss Jane Vernelt--Mademoiselle Vernelt she called herself-- who ran a costumier's business in George Street, in the very building, in fact now occupied by the chemist you have mentioned. The business was for sale, and Miss Vernelt wanted a big sum for it. However, as her books showed a very satisfactory annual increase in receipts and her clientele included a duchess and other society leaders, I considered the bargain a tolerably safe one, and we came to terms. Within a week I was running the business, and, exactly a month after I had taken it over, I was greatly astonished to receive a visit from Miss Vernelt. She came into the shop quite beside herself with agitation. 'It's all a mistake!' she screamed. 'I didn't want to sell it. I can't do anything with my capital. Let me buy it back.' I listened to her politely, and then informed her that as I had gone to all the trouble of taking over the business and had already succeeded in extending it, I most certainly had no intention of selling it--at least not for some time. Well, she behaved like a lunatic, and in the end created such a disturbance that I had to summon my assistants and actually turn her out. After that I had no peace for six weeks. She came every day, at any and all times, and I was at last obliged to take legal proceedings. I then discovered that her mind was really unhinged, and that she had been suffering from softening of the brain for many months. Her medical advisers had, it appeared, warned her to give up business and place herself in the hands of trustworthy friends or relations, who would see that her money was properly invested, but she had delayed doing so; and when, at last, she did make up her mind to retire, the excitement, resulting from so great a change in her mode of living, accelerated the disease, and, exactly three weeks after the sale of her business, she became a victim to the delusion that she was ruined. This delusion grew more and more pronounced as her malady increased, and amidst her wildest ravings she clamoured to be taken back to George Street. The hauntings, indeed, began before she died; and I frequently saw her--when I knew her material body to be under restraint--just as you describe, gliding in and out the show-rooms.

"For several weeks after her death, the manifestations continued--they then ceased, and I have never heard of her again until now."

If I remember rightly the account of the George Street ghost here terminated; but my friend referred to it again at the close of his letter.

"Since my return to Scotland," he wrote, "I have frequently visited George Street, almost daily, but I have not seen 'Jane.' I only hope that her poor distracted spirit has at last found rest." And with this kindly sentiment my correspondent concluded.

CASE V

THE SALLOW-FACED WOMAN OF NO. -- FORREST ROAD, EDINBURGH

The Public unfortunately includes a certain set of people, of the middle class very "middlish," who are ever on the look-out for some opportunity, however slight and seemingly remote, of bettering themselves socially; and, learning that those in a higher strata of society are interested in the supernatural, they think that they may possibly get in touch with them by working up a little local reputation for psychical research. I have often had letters from this type of "pusher" (letters from genuine believers in the Occult I always welcome) stating that they have been greatly interested in my books--would I be so very kind as to grant them a brief interview, or permit them to accompany me to a haunted house, or give them certain information with regard to Lady So-and-so, whom they have long wanted to know? Occasionally, I have been so taken in as to give permission to the writer to call on me, and almost always I have bitterly repented. The wily one--no matter how wily--cannot conceal the cloven hoof for long, and he has either tried to thrust himself into the bosom of my family, or has written to my neighbours declaring himself to be my dearest friend; and when, in desperation, I have shown him the cold shoulder, he has attacked me virulently in some "rag" of a local paper, the proprietor, editor, or office-boy of which happens to be one of his own clique. I have even known an instance where this type of person has, through trickery, actually gained access to some notoriously haunted house, and from its owners--the family he has long had his eyes on, from a motive anything but psychic--has ferreted out the secret and private history of the haunting. Then, when he has been "found out" and forced to see that his friendship is not wanted, he has, in revenge for the slight, unblushingly revealed the facts that were only entrusted to him in the strictest confidence; and, through influence with the lower stratum of the Press, caused a most glaring and sensational account of the ghost to be published.

With such a case in view, I cannot be surprised that possessors of family ghosts and haunted houses should show the greatest reluctance to be approached on the subject, save by those they feel assured will treat it with the utmost delicacy.

But I have quoted the above breach of confidence merely to give another reason for my constant use of fictitious names with regard to people and places, and having done so (I hope to some purpose), I will proceed with the following story:--

Miss Dulcie Vincent, some of whose reminiscences appeared in my book of _Ghostly Phenomena_ last year, is nearly connected with Lady Adela Minkon, who owns a considerable amount of house property, including No. -- Forrest Road, in Edinburgh, and whose yacht at Cowes is the envy of all who have cruised in her. Three years ago, Lady Adela stayed at No. -- Forrest Road. She had heard that the house was haunted, and was anxious to put it to the test. Lady Adela was perfectly open-minded. She had never experienced any occult phenomena herself, but, very rationally, she did not consider that her non-acquaintance with the superphysical in any way negatived the evidence of those who declare that they have witnessed manifestations; their statements, she reasoned, were just as worthy of credence as hers. She thus commenced her occupation of the house with a perfectly unbiased mind, resolved to stay there for at least a year, so as to give it a fair trial. The hauntings, she was told, were at their height in the late summer and early autumn. It is, I think, unnecessary to enter into any detailed description of her house. In appearance, it differed very little, if at all, from those adjoining it; in construction, it was if anything a trifle larger. The basement, which included the usual kitchen offices and cellars, was very dark, and the atmosphere--after sunset on Fridays, only on Fridays--was tainted with a smell of damp earth, shockingly damp earth, and of a sweet and nauseating something that greatly puzzled Lady Adela. All the rooms in the house were of fair dimensions, and cheerful, excepting on this particular evening of the week; a distinct gloom settled on them then, and the strangest of shadows were seen playing about the passages and on the landings.

"It may be fancy," Lady Adela said to herself, "merely fancy! And, after all, if I encounter nothing worse than a weekly menu of aromatic smells and easily digested shadows, I shall not suffer any harm"; but it was early summer then--the psychic season had yet to come. As the weeks went by, the shadows and the smell grew more and more pronounced, and by the arrival of August had become so emphatic that Lady Adela could not help thinking that they were both hostile and aggressive.

About eight o'clock on the evening of the second Friday in the month, Lady Adela was purposely alone in the basement of the house. The servants especially irritated her; like the majority of present-day domestics, products of the County Council schools, they were so intensely supercilious and silly, and Lady Adela felt that their presence in the house minimised her chances of seeing the ghost. No apparition with the smallest amount of self-respect could risk coming in contact with such inane creatures, so she sent them all out for a motor drive, and, for once, rejoiced in the house to herself. A curious proceeding for a lady! True! but then, Lady Adela was a lady, and, being a lady, was not afraid of being thought anything else; and so acted just as unconventionally as she chose. But stay a moment; she was not alone in the house, for she had three of her dogs with her--three beautiful boarhounds, trophies of her last trip to the Baltic. With such colossal and perfectly trained companions Lady Adela felt absolutely safe, and ready--as she acknowledged afterwards--to face a whole army of spooks. She did not even shiver when the front door of the basement closed, and she heard the sonorous birring of the motor, drowning the giddy voices of the servants, grow fainter and fainter until it finally ceased altogether.

When the last echoes of the vehicle had died away in the distance, Lady Adela made a tour of the premises. The housekeeper's room pleased her immensely--at least she persuaded herself it did. "Why, it is quite as nice as any of the rooms upstairs," she said aloud, as she stood with her face to the failing sunbeams and rested her strong white hand on the edge of the table. "Quite as nice. Karl and Max, come here!"

But the boarhounds for once in their lives did not obey her with a good grace. There was something in the room they did not like, and they showed how strong was their resentment by slinking unwillingly through the doorway.

"I wonder why that is?" Lady Adela mused; "I have never known them do it before." Then her eyes wandered round the walls, and struggled in vain to reach the remoter angles of the room, which had suddenly grown dark. She tried to assure herself that this was but the natural effect of the departing daylight, and that, had she watched in other houses at this particular time, she would have noticed the same thing. To show how little she minded the gloom, she went up to the darkest corner and prodded the walls with her riding-whip. She laughed--there was nothing there, nothing whatsoever to be afraid of, only shadows. With a careless shrug of her shoulders, she strutted into the passage, and, whistling to Karl and Max who, contrary to their custom, would not keep to heel, made another inspection of the kitchens. At the top of the cellar steps she halted. The darkness had now set in everywhere, and she argued that it would be foolish to venture into such dungeon-like places without a light. She soon found one, and, armed with candle and matches, began her descent. There were several cellars, and they presented such a dismal, dark appearance, that she instinctively drew her skirts tightly round her, and exchanged the slender riding-whip for a poker. She whistled again to her dogs. They did not answer, so she called them both by name angrily. But for some reason (some quite unaccountable reason, she told herself) they would not come.

She ransacked her mind to recall some popular operatic air, and although she knew scores she could not remember one. Indeed, the only air that filtered back to her was one she detested--a Vaudeville tune she had heard three nights in succession, when she was staying with a student friend in the Latin Quarter in Paris. She hummed it loudly, however, and, holding the lighted candle high above her head, walked down the steps. At the bottom she stood still and listened. From high above her came noises which sounded like the rumbling of distant thunder, but which, on analysis, proved to be the rattling of window-frames. Reassured that she had no cause for alarm, Lady Adela advanced. Something black scudded across the red-tiled floor, and she made a dash at it with her poker. The concussion awoke countless echoes in the cellars, and called into existence legions of other black things that darted hither and thither in all directions. She burst out laughing--they were only beetles! Facing her she now perceived an inner cellar, which was far gloomier than the one in which she stood. The ceiling was very low, and appeared to be crushed down beneath the burden of a stupendous weight; and as she advanced beneath it she half expected that it would "cave in" and bury her.

A few feet from the centre of this cellar she stopped; and, bending down, examined the floor carefully. The tiles were unmistakably newer here than elsewhere, and presented the appearance of having been put in at no very distant date. The dampness of the atmosphere was intense; a fact which struck Lady Adela as somewhat odd, since the floor and walls looked singularly dry. To find out if this were the case, she ran her fingers over the walls, and, on removing them, found they showed no signs of moisture. Then she rapped the floor and walls, and could discover no indications of hollowness. She sniffed the air, and a great wave of something sweet and sickly half choked her. She drew out her handkerchief and beat the air vigorously with it; but the smell remained, and she could not in any way account for it. She turned to leave the cellar, and the flame of her candle burned blue. Then for the first time that evening--almost, indeed, for the first time in her life--she felt afraid, so afraid that she made no attempt to diagnose her fear; she understood the dogs' feelings now, and caught herself wondering how much they knew.

She whistled to them again, not because she thought they would respond,--she knew only too well they would not,--but because she wanted company, even the company of her own voice; and she had some faint hope, too, that whatever might be with her in the cellar, would not so readily disclose itself if she made a noise. The one cellar was passed, and she was nearly across the floor of the other when she heard a crash. The candle dropped from her hand, and all the blood in her body rushed to her heart. She could never have imagined it was so terrible to be frightened. She tried to pull herself together and be calm, but she was no longer mistress of her limbs. Her knees knocked together and her hands shook. "It was only the dogs," she feebly told herself, "I will call them"; but when she opened her mouth, she found her throat was paralysed--not a syllable would come. She knew, too, that she had lied, and that the hounds could not have been responsible for the noise. It was like nothing she had ever heard, nothing she could imagine; and although she struggled hard against the idea, she could not help associating the sound with the cause of the candle burning blue, and the sweet, sickly smell. Incapable of moving a step, she was forced to listen in breathless expectancy for a recurrence of the crash. Her thoughts become ghastly. The inky sea of darkness that hemmed her in on every side suggested every sort of ghoulish possibility, and with each pulsation of her overstrained heart her flesh crawled. Another sound--this time not a crash, nothing half so loud or definite--drew her eyes in the direction of the steps. An object was now standing at the top of them, and something lurid, like the faint, phosphorescent glow of decay, emanated from all over it; but _what_ it was, she could not for the life of her tell. It might have been the figure of a man, or a woman, or a beast, or of anything that was inexpressibly antagonistic and nasty. She would have given her soul to have looked elsewhere, but her eyes were fixed--she could neither turn nor shut them. For some seconds the shape remained motionless, and then with a sly, subtle motion it lowered its head, and came stealing stealthily down the stairs towards her. She followed its approach like one in a hideous dream--her heart ready to burst, her brain on the verge of madness. Another step, another, yet another; till there were only three left between her and it; and she was at length enabled to form some idea of what the thing was like.

It was short and squat, and appeared to be partly clad in a loose, flowing garment, that was not long enough to conceal the glistening extremities of its limbs. From its general contour and the tangled mass of hair that fell about its neck and shoulders, Lady Adela concluded it was the phantasm of a woman. Its head being kept bent, she was unable to see the face in full, but every instant she expected the revelation would take place, and with each separate movement of the phantasm her suspense became more and more intolerable. At last it stood on the floor of the cellar, a broad, ungainly, horribly ungainly figure, that glided up to and past her into the far cellar. There it halted, as nearly as she could judge on the new tiles, and remained standing. As she gazed at it, too fascinated to remove her eyes, there was a loud, reverberating crash, a hideous sound of wrenching and tearing, and the whole of the ceiling of the inner chamber came down with an appalling roar. Lady Adela thinks that she must then have fainted, for she distinctly remembers falling--falling into what seemed to her a black, interminable abyss. When she recovered consciousness, she was lying on the tiles, and all around was still and normal. She got up, found and lighted her candle, and spent the rest of the evening, without further adventure, in the drawing-room.

All the week Lady Adela struggled hard to master a disinclination to spend another evening alone in the house, and when Friday came she succumbed to her fears. The servants were poor, foolish things, but it was nice to feel that there was something in the house besides ghosts. She sat reading in the drawing-room till late that night, and when she lolled out of the window to take a farewell look at the sky and stars before retiring to rest, the sounds of traffic had completely ceased and the whole city lay bathed in a refreshing silence. It was very heavenly to stand there and feel the cool, soft air--unaccompanied, for the first time during the day, by the rattling rumbling sounds of locomotion and the jarring discordant murmurs of unmusical voices--fanning her neck and face.

Lady Adela, used as she was to the privacy of her yacht, and the freedom of her big country mansion, where all sounds were regulated at her will, chafed at the near proximity of her present habitation to the noisy thoroughfare, and vaguely looked forward to the hours when shops and theatres were closed, and all screeching, harsh-voiced products of the gutter were in bed. To her the nights in Waterloo Place were all too short; the days too long, too long for anything. The heavy, lumbering steps of a policeman at last broke her reverie. She had no desire to arouse his curiosity; besides, her costume had become somewhat disordered, and she had the strictest sense of propriety, at least in the presence of the lower orders. Retiring, therefore, with a sigh of vexation, she sought her bedroom, and, after the most scrupulous attention to her toilet, put out the lights and got into bed. It was just one when she fell asleep, and three when she awoke with a violent start. Why she started puzzled her. She did not recollect experiencing any very dreadful dream, in fact no dream at all, and there seemed nothing in the hush--the apparently unbroken hush--that could in any way account for her action. Why, then, had she started? She lay still and wondered. Surely everything was just as it was when she went to sleep! And yet! When she ventured on a diagnosis, there was something different, something new; she did not think it was actually in the atmosphere, nor in the silence; she did not know where it was until she opened her eyes--and then she _knew_. Bending over her, within a few inches of her face, was another face, the ghastly caricature of a human face. It was on a larger scale than that of any mortal Lady Adela had ever seen; it was long in proportion to its width--indeed, she could not make out where the cranium terminated at the back, as the hinder portion of it was lost in a mist. The forehead, which was very receding, was partly covered with a mass of lank, black hair, that fell straight down into space; there were no neck nor shoulders, at least none had materialised; the skin was leaden-hued, and the emaciation so extreme that the raw cheek-bones had burst through in places; the size of the eye sockets which appeared monstrous, was emphasised by the fact that the eyes were considerably sunken; the lips were curled downwards and tightly shut, and the whole expression of the withered mouth, as indeed that of the entire face, was one of bestial, diabolical malignity. Lady Adela's heart momentarily stopped, her blood ran cold, she was petrified; and as she stared helplessly at the dark eyes pressed close to hers, she saw them suddenly suffuse with fiendish glee. The most frightful change then took place: the upper lip writhed away from a few greenish yellow stumps; the lower jaw fell with a metallic click, leaving the mouth widely open, and disclosing to Lady Adela's shocked vision a black and bloated tongue; the eyeballs rolled up and entirely disappeared, whilst their places were immediately filled with the foulest and most loathsome indications of advanced decay. A strong, vibratory movement suddenly made all the bones in the head rattle and the tongue wag, whilst from the jaws, as if belched up from some deep-down well, came a gust of wind, putrescent with the ravages of the tomb, and yet, at the same time, tainted with the same sweet, sickly odour with which Lady Adela had latterly become so familiar. This was the culminating act; the head then receded, and, growing fainter and fainter, gradually disappeared altogether. Lady Adela was now more than satisfied,--there was not a house more horribly haunted in Scotland,--and nothing on earth would induce her to remain in it another night.

However, being anxious, naturally, to discover something that might, in some degree, account for the apparitions, Lady Adela made endless inquiries concerning the history of former occupants of the house; but, failing to find out anything remarkable in this direction, she was eventually obliged to content herself with the following tradition: It was said that on the site of No. -- Forrest Road there had once stood a cottage occupied by two sisters (both nurses), and that one was suspected of poisoning the other; and that the cottage, moreover, having through their parsimonious habits got into a very bad state of repair, was blown down during a violent storm, the surviving sister perishing in the ruins. Granted that this story is correct, it was in all probability the ghost of this latter sister that appeared to Lady Adela. Her ladyship is, of course, anxious to let No. -- Forrest Road, and as only about one in a thousand people seem to possess the faculty of seeing psychic phenomena, she hopes she may one day succeed in getting a permanent tenant. In the meanwhile, she is doing her level best to suppress the rumour that the house is haunted.

CASE VI

THE PHANTOM REGIMENT OF KILLIECRANKIE

Many are the stories that have from time to time been circulated with regard to the haunting of the Pass of Killiecrankie by phantom soldiers, but I do not think there is any stranger story than that related to me, some years ago, by a lady who declared she had actually witnessed the phenomena. Her account of it I shall reproduce as far as possible in her own words:--

* * * * *

Let me commence by stating that I am not a spiritualist, and that I have the greatest possible aversion to convoking the earthbound souls of the dead. Neither do I lay any claim to mediumistic powers (indeed I have always regarded the term "medium" with the gravest suspicion). I am, on the contrary, a plain, practical, matter-of-fact woman, and with the exception of this one occasion, never witnessed any psychic phenomena.

The incident I am about to relate took place the autumn before last. I was on a cycle tour in Scotland, and, making Pitlochry my temporary headquarters, rode over one evening to view the historic Pass of Killiecrankie. It was late when I arrived there, and the western sky was one great splash of crimson and gold--such vivid colouring I had never seen before and never have seen since. Indeed, I was so entranced at the sublimity of the spectacle, that I perched myself on a rock at the foot of one of the great cliffs that form the walls of the Pass, and, throwing my head back, imagined myself in fairyland. Lost, thus, in a delicious luxury, I paid no heed to the time, nor did I think of stirring, until the dark shadows of the night fell across my face. I then started up in a panic, and was about to pedal off in hot haste, when a strange notion suddenly seized me: I had a latchkey, plenty of sandwiches, a warm cape, why should I not camp out there till early morning--I had long yearned to spend a night in the open, now was my opportunity. The idea was no sooner conceived than put into operation. Selecting the most comfortable-looking boulder I could see, I scrambled on to the top of it, and, with my cloak drawn tightly over my back and shoulders, commenced my vigil. The cold mountain air, sweet with the perfume of gorse and heather, intoxicated me, and I gradually sank into a heavenly torpor, from which I was abruptly aroused by a dull boom, that I at once associated with distant musketry. All was then still, still as the grave, and, on glancing at the watch I wore strapped on my wrist, I saw it was two o'clock. A species of nervous dread now laid hold of me, and a thousand and one vague fancies, all the more distressing because of their vagueness, oppressed and disconcerted me. Moreover, I was impressed for the first time with the extraordinary solitude--solitude that seemed to belong to a period far other than the present, and, as I glanced around at the solitary pines and gleaming boulders, I more than half expected to see the wild, ferocious face of some robber chief-- some fierce yet fascinating hero of Sir Walter Scott's-- peering at me from behind them. This feeling at length became so acute, that, in a panic of fear-- ridiculous, puerile fear, I forcibly withdrew my gaze and concentrated it abstractedly on the ground at my feet. I then listened, and in the rustling of a leaf, the humming of some night insect, the whizzing of a bat, the whispering of the wind as it moaned softly past me, I fancied--nay, I felt sure I detected something that was not ordinary. I blew my nose, and had barely ceased marvelling at the loudness of its reverberations, before the piercing, ghoulish shriek of an owl sent the blood in torrents to my heart. I then laughed, and my blood froze as I heard a chorus, of what I tried to persuade myself could only be echoes, proceed from every crag and rock in the valley. For some seconds after this I sat still, hardly daring to breathe, and pretending to be extremely angry with myself for being such a fool. With a stupendous effort I turned my attention to the most material of things. One of the skirt buttons on my hip--they were much in vogue then--being loose, I endeavoured to occupy myself in tightening it, and when I could no longer derive any employment from that, I set to work on my shoes, and tied knots in the laces, merely to enjoy the task of untying them. But this, too, ceasing at last to attract me, I was desperately racking my mind for some other device, when there came again the queer, booming noise I had heard before, but which I could now no longer doubt was the report of firearms. I looked in the direction of the sound--and--my heart almost stopped. Racing towards me--as if not merely for his life, but his soul--came the figure of a Highlander. The wind rustling through his long dishevelled hair, blew it completely over his forehead, narrowly missing his eyes, which were fixed ahead of him in a ghastly, agonised stare. He had not a vestige of colour, and, in the powerful glow of the moonbeams, his skin shone livid. He ran with huge bounds, and, what added to my terror and made me double aware he was nothing mortal, was that each time his feet struck the hard, smooth road, upon which I could well see there was no sign of a stone, there came the sound, the unmistakable sound of the scattering of gravel. On, on he came, with cyclonic swiftness; his bare sweating elbows pressed into his panting sides; his great, dirty, coarse, hairy fists screwed up in bony bunches in front of him; the foam-flakes thick on his clenched, grinning lips; the blood-drops oozing down his sweating thighs. It was all real, infernally, hideously real, even to the most minute details: the flying up and down of his kilt, sporan, and swordless scabbard; the bursting of the seam of his coat, near the shoulder; and the absence of one of his clumsy shoe-buckles. I tried hard to shut my eyes, but was compelled to keep them open, and follow his every movement as, darting past me, he left the roadway, and, leaping several of the smaller obstacles that barred his way, finally disappeared behind some of the bigger boulders. I then heard the loud rat-tat of drums, accompanied by the shrill voices of fifes and flutes, and at the farther end of the Pass, their arms glittering brightly in the silvery moonbeams, appeared a regiment of scarlet-clad soldiers. At the head rode a mounted officer, after him came the band, and then, four abreast, a long line of warriors; in their centre two ensigns, and on their flanks, officers and non-commissioned officers with swords and pikes; more mounted men bringing up the rear. On they came, the fifes and flutes ringing out with a weird clearness in the hushed mountain air. I could hear the ground vibrate, the gravel crunch and scatter, as they steadily and mechanically advanced--tall men, enormously tall men, with set, white faces and livid eyes. Every instant

I expected they would see me, and I became sick with terror at the thought of meeting all those pale, flashing eyes. But from this I was happily saved; no one appeared to notice me, and they all passed me by without as much as a twist or turn of the head, their feet keeping time to one everlasting and monotonous tramp, tramp, tramp. I got up and watched until the last of them had turned the bend of the Pass, and the sheen of his weapons and trappings could no longer be seen; then I remounted my boulder and wondered if anything further would happen. It was now half-past two, and blended with the moonbeams was a peculiar whiteness, which rendered the whole aspect of my surroundings indescribably dreary and ghostly. Feeling cold and hungry, I set to work on my beef sandwiches, and was religiously separating the fat from the lean, for I am one of those foolish people who detest fat, when a loud rustling made me look up. Confronting me, on the opposite side of the road, was a tree, an ash, and to my surprise, despite the fact that the breeze had fallen and there was scarcely a breath of wind, the tree swayed violently to and fro, whilst there proceeded from it the most dreadful moanings and groanings. I was so terrified that I caught hold of my bicycle and tried to mount, but I was obliged to desist as I had not a particle of strength in my limbs. Then to assure myself the moving of the tree was not an illusion, I rubbed my eyes, pinched myself, called aloud; but it made no difference--the rustling, bending, and tossing still continued. Summing up courage, I stepped into the road to get a closer view, when to my horror my feet kicked against something, and, on looking down, I perceived the body of an English soldier, with a ghastly wound in his chest. I gazed around, and there, on all sides of me, from one end of the valley to the other, lay dozens of bodies,--bodies of men and horses,--Highlanders and English, white-cheeked, lurid eyes, and bloody-browed,--a hotch-potch of livid, gory awfulness. Here was the writhing, wriggling figure of an officer with half his face shot away; and there, a horse with no head; and there--but I cannot dwell on such horrors, the very memory of which makes me feel sick and faint. The air, that beautiful, fresh mountain air, resounded with their moanings and groanings, and reeked with the smell of their blood. As I stood rooted to the ground with horror, not knowing which way to look or turn, I suddenly saw drop from the ash, the form of a woman, a Highland girl, with bold, handsome features, raven black hair, and the whitest of arms and feet. In one hand she carried a wicker basket, in the other a knife, a broad-bladed, sharp-edged, horn-handled knife. A gleam of avarice and cruelty came into her large dark eyes, as, wandering around her, they rested on the rich facings of the English officers' uniforms. I knew what was in her mind, and--forgetting she was but a ghost--that they were all ghosts--I moved heaven and earth to stop her. I could not. Making straight for a wounded officer that lay moaning piteously on the ground, some ten feet away from me, she spurned with her slender, graceful feet, the bodies of the dead and dying English that came in her way. Then, snatching the officer's sword and pistol from him, she knelt down, and, with a look of devilish glee in her glorious eyes, calmly plunged her knife into his heart, working the blade backwards and forwards to assure herself she had made a thorough job of it. Anything more hellish I could not have imagined, and yet it fascinated me--the girl was so fair, so wickedly fair and shapely. Her act of cruelty over, she spoiled her victim of his rings, epaulets, buttons and gold lacing, and, having placed them in her basket, proceeded elsewhere. In some cases, unable to remove the rings easily, she chopped off the fingers, and popped them, just as they were, into her basket. Neither was her mode of dispatch always the same, for while she put some men out of their misery in the manner I have described, she cut the throats of others with as great a nonchalance as if she had been killing fowls, whilst others again she settled with the butt-ends of their guns or pistols. In all she murdered a full half-score, and was decamping with her booty when her gloating eyes suddenly encountered mine, and with a shrill scream of rage she rushed towards me. I was an easy victim, for strain and pray how I would, I could not move an inch. Raising her flashing blade high over her head, an expression of fiendish glee in her staring eyes, she made ready to strike me. This was the climax, my overstrained nerves could stand no more, and ere the blow had time to descend, I pitched heavily forward and fell at her feet. When I recovered, every phantom had vanished, and the Pass glowed with all the cheerful freshness of the early morning sun. Not a whit the worse for my venture, I cycled swiftly home, and ate as only one can eat who has spent the night amid the banks and braes of bonnie Scotland.

CASE VII

"PEARLIN' JEAN" OF ALLANBANK

Few ghosts have obtained more notoriety than "Pearlin' Jean," the phantasm which for many years haunted Allanbank, a seat of the Stuarts.

The popular theory as to the identity of the apparition is as follows:--

Mr. Stuart, afterwards created first baronet of Allanbank, when on a tour in France, met a young and beautiful French Sister of Charity of the name of Jean, whom he induced to leave her convent. Tiring of her at length, Mr. Stuart brutally left her, and, returning abruptly to Scotland, became engaged to be married to a lady of his own nationality and position in life. But Jean was determined he should not escape her so easily. For him she had sacrificed everything: her old vocation in life was gone, she had no home, no honour,--nothing, so she resolved to leave no stone unturned to discover his whereabouts. At last her perseverance was rewarded, and, Fortune favouring her, she arrived without mishap at Allanbank.

The truth was then revealed to her: her cruel and faithless lover was about to be wedded to another. But despair gave her energy, and, burning with indignation, she hastened to his house to upbraid him. She reached the spot just as he was driving out with his fiancée. With a cry of anguish, Jean rushed forward and, swinging herself nimbly on to the fore-wheel of the coach, turned her white and passionate face towards its occupants. For a moment, Mr. Stuart was too dumbfounded to do anything; he could scarcely believe his senses. Who on earth was this frantic female? Good Heavens! Jean! Impossible! How on earth had she got there? And the tumultuous beating of his guilty heart turned him sick and faint.

Then he glanced fearfully and covertly at his fiancée. _She_ must not know the truth at any cost. Possibly he lost his head! At all events, that is the kindest construction to put on his subsequent action, for, dastardly as his behaviour had been to Jean in the past, one can hardly imagine him capable of deliberately murdering her, and in so horrible a fashion. There was not a second to lose; an instant more, and the secret, that he had so assiduously hidden from the lady beside him, would be revealed. Jean's mouth was already open to speak. He waved her aside. She adhered to her post. He shouted to the

68

postilion, and the huge, lumbering vehicle was set in motion. At the first turn of the wheels, Jean slipped from her perch, her dress caught in the spokes, and she was crushed to death.

Her fate does not appear to have made any deep impression either on Mr. Stuart or his lady-love, for they continued their drive.

The hauntings began that autumn. Mr. Stuart, as was only fit and proper, being the first to witness the phenomenon. Returning home from a drive one evening, he perceived to his surprise the dark outlines of a human figure perched on the arched gateway of his house, exactly opposite the spot where Jean had perished. Wondering who it could be, he leaned forward to inspect it closer. The figure moved, an icy current of air ran through him, and he saw to his horror the livid countenance of the dead Jean. There she was, staring down at him with lurid, glassy eyes; her cheeks startlingly white, her hair fluttering in the wind, her neck and forehead bathed in blood.

Paralysed with terror, Mr. Stuart could not remove his gaze, and it was not until one of the menials opened the carriage door to assist him down, that the spell was broken and he was able to speak and move. He then flew into the house, and spent the rest of the night in the most abject fear.

After this he had no peace--Allanbank was constantly haunted. The great oak doors opened and shut of their own accord at night with loud clanging and bangs, and the rustling of silks and pattering of high-heeled shoes were heard in the oak-panelled bedrooms and along the many dark and winding passages.

From her attire, which was a piece of lace made of thread, the apparition became known as "Pearlin' Jean," and a portrait of her was actually painted. It is recorded that when this picture was hung between one of Mr. Stuart and his lady-love, the hauntings ceased, but that as soon as it was removed they were renewed. Presumably, it was not allowed to remain in the aforesaid position long, for the manifestations appear to have gone on for many years without intermission.

Most phantasms of the dead inspire those who see them with horror,--and that is my own experience,--but "Pearlin' Jean" seems to have been an exception to this rule. A housekeeper called Betty Norrie, who lived for many years at Allanbank, declared that other people besides herself had so frequently seen Jean that they had grown quite accustomed to her, and were, consequently, no more alarmed at her appearance than they were by her noises.

Another servant at the house, of the name of Jenny Blackadder, used constantly to hear Jean, but could never see her--though her husband did.

The latter, when courting Jenny, received a rare scare, which suggests to me that Jean, in spite of her tragic ending, may not have been without a spice of humour. Thomas, for that was the swain's name, made an assignation one night to meet Jenny in the orchard at Allanbank.

It was early when he arrived at the trysting-place--for Thomas, like all true lovers, was ever rather more than punctual--and he fully contemplated a long wait. Judge, then, of his astonishment, when he perceived in the moonlight what he took to be the well-known and adored figure of his lady-love. With a cry of delight, Thomas rushed forward, and, swinging his arms widely open to embrace her, beheld her vanish, and found himself hugging space! An icy current of air thrilled through him, and the whole place--trees, nooks, moonbeams, and shadows, underwent a hideous metamorphosis. The very air bristled with unknown horrors till flesh and blood could stand no more, and, even at the risk of displeasing his beloved Jenny, Thomas fled! Some few minutes later, at the appointed hour, Jenny arrived on the scene, and no one was there. She dallied for some time, wondering whatever could have happened to Thomas, and then returned, full of grave apprehensions, to the house.

It was not until the next morning that the truth leaked out, and Jenny, after indulging in a hearty laugh at her lover, who felt very shamefaced now that it was daylight, sensibly forgave him, and raised no obstacle when asked to fix a day for their marriage.

In after years, Jenny used to retail the story with many harrowing allusions to "Pearlin' Jean," whom she somewhat foolishly made use of as a bogey to frighten children into being good. A Mr. Sharpe, who when he was a little boy was once placed in her charge, confesses that he was dreadfully scared at her stories, and that he never ventured down a passage in those days without thinking "Pearlin' Jean," with her ghostly, blood-stained face, clawlike hands, and rustling lace dress, was after him.

Nurse Jenny used to tell him that the Stuarts tried in vain to lay Jean's spirit, actually going to the length of calling in seven ministers to exorcise it. But all to no purpose; it still continued its nocturnal peregrinations.

In the year 1790 the Stuarts let the house to strangers, who, when they took it, had not the least idea that it was haunted. However, they did not long remain in ignorance, for two ladies, who occupied the same bedroom, were awakened in the night by hearing some one walking across the floor. The "presence" did not suggest burglars, for the intruder behaved in the most noisy manner, pacing restlessly and apparently aimlessly backwards and forwards across the room, swishing the floor (with what sounded like a long lace train) and breathing heavily. They were both terrified, and so cold that they could hear one another's teeth chatter. They were too frightened to call for help; they could only lie still, hoping and praying it would not come nearer to them. The sufferings of these two ladies were indescribable, for the ghost remained in their room all night, moving restlessly about until daybreak. It was not until some days later, when other people in the house had experienced the phenomenon, that they were told the story of the notorious "Pearlin' Jean."

But was the so-called "Pearlin' Jean" really the apparition of the murdered French woman? To my mind, her identity with that of the beautiful Sister of Charity has not been satisfactorily established, and I think there are reasons to doubt it.

If, for instance, the apparition were that of a Sister of Charity, why should it appear incongruously attired in a long trailing gown of lace? And if it were that of a woman of the presumably staid habits of a Sister of Charity, why should it delight in mischief and play the pranks of a _poltergeist_? And yet if it wasn't the ghost of Jean, whose ghost was it?

CASE VIII

THE DRUMMER OF CORTACHY

What ancient Scottish or Irish family has not its Family Ghost? A banshee--the heritage of Niall of the Nine Hostages--is still the unenviable possession of his descendants, the O'Donnells, and I, who am a member of the clan, have both seen and heard it several times. As it appears to me, it resembles the decapitated head of a prehistoric woman, and I shall never forget my feelings one night, when, aroused from slumber by its ghastly wailing, I stumbled frantically out of bed, and, groping my way upstairs in the dark, without venturing to look to the left or right lest I should see something horrible, found every inmate of the house huddled together on the landing, paralysed with fear. I did not see it on that occasion, but on the following morning, as I had anticipated, I received the news that a near and dear relative had died.

Possessing such an heirloom myself, I can therefore readily sympathise with those who own a similar treasure--such, for example, as the famous, or rather infamous, Drummer of Cortachy Castle, who is invariably heard beating a tattoo before the death of a member of the clan of Ogilvie.

Mrs. Crowe, in her _Night Side of Nature_, referring to the haunting, says:--

"Miss D., a relative of the present Lady C., who had been staying some time with the Earl and Countess at their seat, near Dundee, was invited to spend a few days at Cortachy Castle, with the Earl and Countess of Airlie. She went, and whilst she was dressing for dinner the first evening of her arrival, she heard a strain of music under her window, which finally resolved itself into a well-defined sound of a drum. When her maid came upstairs, she made some inquiries about the drummer that was playing near the house; but the maid knew nothing on the subject.

For the moment the circumstance passed from Miss D.'s mind, but, recurring to her again during the dinner, she said, addressing Lord Airlie, 'My lord, who is your drummer?' Upon which his lordship turned pale, Lady Airlie looked distressed, and several of the company, who all heard the question, embarrassed; whilst the lady, perceiving that she had made some unpleasant allusion, although she knew not to what their feelings referred, forebore further inquiry till she reached the drawing-room; when, having mentioned the circumstance again to a member of the family, she was answered, 'What, have you never heard of the drummer boy?' 'No,' replied Miss D.; 'who in the world is he?' 'Why,' replied the other, 'he is a person who goes about the house playing his drum, whenever there is a death impending in the family. The last time he was heard was shortly before the death of the last Countess (the Earl's former wife); and that is why Lord Airlie became so pale when you mentioned it. The drummer boy is a very unpleasant subject in this family, I assure you.'

"Miss D. was naturally much concerned, and indeed not a little frightened at this explanation, and her alarm being augmented by hearing the sounds on the following day, she took her departure from Cortachy Castle, and returned to Lord C.'s, where she related this strange circumstance to the family, through whom the information reached me.

"This affair was very generally known in the north, and we awaited the event with interest. The

75

melancholy death of the Countess about five or six months afterwards, at Brighton, sadly verified the prognostications. I have heard that a paper was found in her desk after her death, declaring her conviction that the drum was for her."

Mrs. Crowe goes on to explain the origin of the phenomenon. According to legend, she says, there was once at Cortachy a drummer, who, incurring the jealousy of the then Lord Airlie, was thrust into his own drum and flung from a window of the tower (in which, by the way, Miss D. slept). Before being put to death thus, the drummer is stated to have said he would for ever after haunt the Airlie family--a threat he has obviously been permitted to fulfil.

During one of my visits to Scotland, I stayed some days in Forfarshire not far from Cortachy. Among the visitors at my hotel was a very old gentleman of the name of Porter, who informed me that, when a boy, he used to visit some relatives who, at that time, lived within easy walking distance of Cortachy. One of these relatives was a lad of about fourteen, named Alec, with whom he had always been the closest of friends. The recollection of their many adventures evidently afforded Mr. Porter infinite amusement, and one of these adventures, in particular, he told me, was as fresh in his mind as if it had happened yesterday.

"Looking back upon it now," he said, with a far-away look in his eyes, "it certainly was a strange coincidence, and if you are interested in the hauntings of Cortachy, Mr. O'Donnell, you may, perhaps, like to hear the account of my ghostly experiences in that neighbourhood."

Of course I replied that nothing would give me greater pleasure, and Mr. Porter forthwith began his story.

"One misty night in October, my friend Alec and I, both being keen on rabbiting, determined to visit a spinney adjoining the Cortachy estate, in pursuit of our quarry. Alec had chosen this particular night, thinking, under cover of the mist, to escape the vigilance of the keepers, who had more than once threatened to take him before the laird for trespassing.

"To gain access to the spinney we had to climb a granite wall and drop on the other side--the drop, in addition to being steep, being rendered all the more precarious by reason of the man-traps the keepers were in the habit of setting. When I got astride the wall and peered into the well-like darkness at our feet, and heard the grim rustling of the wind through the giant pines ahead of me, I would have given all I possessed to have found myself snug and warm in bed; but Alec was of a different 'kidney'--he had come prepared for excitement, and he meant to have it. For some seconds, we both waited on the wall in breathless silence, and then Alec, with a reckless disregard of what might be in store for him, gently let himself drop, and I, fearing more, if anything, than the present danger, to be for ever after branded as a coward if I held back, timidly followed suit. By a great stroke of luck we alighted in safety on a soft carpeting of moss. Not a word was spoken, but, falling on hands and knees, and guiding ourselves by means of a dark lantern Alec had bought second-hand from the village blacksmith, we crept on all-fours along a tiny bramble-covered path, that after innumerable windings eventually brought us into a broad glade shut in on all sides by lofty trees. Alec prospected the spot first of all to see no keepers were about, and we then crawled into it, and, approaching the nearest burrows, set to work at once with our ferrets. Three rabbits were captured in this fashion, and we were eagerly anticipating the taking of more, when a sensation of icy coldness suddenly stole over us, and, on looking round, we perceived, to our utmost consternation, a very tall keeper standing only a few yards away from us. For once in a way, Alec was nonplussed, and a deathly silence ensued. It was too dark for us to see the figure of the keeper very distinctly, and we could only distinguish a gleaming white face set on a very slight and perpendicular frame, and a round, glittering something that puzzled us both exceedingly. Then, a feeling that, perhaps, it was not a keeper gradually stole over me, and in a paroxysm of ungovernable terror I caught hold of Alec, who was trembling from head to foot as if he had the ague. The figure remained absolutely still for about a minute, during which time neither Alec nor I could move a muscle, and then, turning round with an abrupt movement, came towards us.

"Half-dead with fright, but only too thankful to find that we had now regained the use of our limbs, we left our spoil and ran for our lives in the direction of the wall.

"We dared not look back, but we knew the figure followed us, for we heard its footsteps close at our heels; and never to my dying day shall I forget the sound--rat-tat, tat, rat-tat, tat--for all the world like the beat of a muffled drum.

"How we ever managed to reach the wall I could never tell, but as we scrambled over it, regardless of man-traps and bruises, and plunged into the heather on the other side, we heard the weird footsteps receding in the direction of the castle, and, ere we had reached home, the rat-tat, tat, rat-tat, tat, had completely died away.

"We told no one a word of what had happened, and a few days after, simultaneously with the death of one of the Airlies, we learned, for the first time, the story of the Phantom Drummer.

"I have little doubt," Mr. Porter added, in conclusion, "that the figure we took to be a keeper was the prophetic Drummer, for I can assure you there was no possibility of hoaxers, especially in such ill-omened guise, anywhere near the Cortachy estate."

Poor old Mr. Porter! He did not long survive our _rencontre_. When I next visited the hotel, some months later, I was genuinely grieved to hear of his decease. His story had greatly fascinated me, for I love the solitude of the pines, and have myself from time to time witnessed many remarkable occult phenomena under the shadow of their lofty summits. One night, during this second visit of mine to the hotel, the mood to ramble came upon me, and, unable to resist the seductive thought of a midnight stroll across the bracken-covered hills, I borrowed a latchkey, and, armed with a flask of whisky and a thick stick, plunged into the moonlit night. The keen, heather-scented air acted like a tonic--I felt younger and stronger than I had felt for years, and I congratulated myself that my friends would hardly know me if they saw me now, as I swung along with the resuscitated stride of twenty years ago. The landscape for miles around stood out with startling clearness in the moonshine, and I stopped every now and then to drink in the beauties of the glittering mountain-ranges and silent, glimmering tarns. Not a soul was about, and I found myself, as I loved to be, the only human element in the midst of nature. Every now and then a dark patch fluttered across the shining road, and with a weird and plaintive cry, a night bird dashed abruptly from hedge to hedge, and seemingly melted into nothingness. I quitted the main road on the brow of a low hill, and embarked upon a wild expanse of moor, lavishly covered with bracken and white heather, intermingled with which were the silvery surfaces of many a pool of water. For some seconds I stood still, lost in contemplating the scenery,--its utter abandonment and grand sense of isolation; and inhaling at the same time long and deep draughts of the delicious moorland air, unmistakably impregnated now with breaths of ozone. My eyes wandering to the horizon, I detected, on the very margin of the moorland, a dense clump of trees, which I instantly associated with the spinney in my old friend Mr. Porter's story, and, determining that the renowned spinney should be my goal, I at once aimed for it, vigorously striking out along the path which I thought would be most likely to lead to it. Half an hour's brisk walking brought me to my destination, and I found myself standing opposite a granite wall which my imagination had no difficulty in identifying with the wall so well described by Mr. Porter. Removing the briars and gorse prickles which left little of my stockings whole, I went up to the wall, and, measuring it with my body, found it was a good foot taller than I. This would mean rather more climbing than I had bargained for. But the pines--the grim silence of their slender frames and gently swaying summits--fascinated me. They spoke of possibilities few could see or appreciate as I could; possibilities of a sylvan phantasmagoria enhanced by the soft and mystic radiance of the moon. An owl hooted, and the rustling of brushwood told me of the near proximity of some fur-coated burrower in the ground. High above this animal life, remoter even than the tops of my beloved trees or the mountain-ranges, etched on the dark firmament, shone multitudinous stars, even the rings round Saturn being plainly discernible. From the Milky Way my eyes at length wandered to the pines, and a puff of air laden with the odour of their resin and decaying brushwood decided me. I took a few preliminary sips of whisky, stretched my rusty limbs, and, placing one foot in a jagged crevice of the wall, swarmed painfully up. How slow and how hazardous was the process! I scratched my fingers, inured to the pen but a stranger to any rougher substance; I ruined my box-calf boots, I split my trousers at the knees, and I felt that my hat had parted with its shape for ever; and yet I continued the ascent. The end came all too suddenly. When within an ace of victory, I yielded to impulse, and with an energy the desperate condition of my skin and clothes alone could account for, I swung up, and--the outer edge of the wall melted beneath me, my hands frantically clutched at nothingness, a hideous sensation of falling surged through my brain, my ears and eyes filled to bursting, and with a terrific crash that seemed to drive my head and spine right through my stomach, I met the black, uprising earth, and lost consciousness.

Providentially for me, I had pitched head first into a furze bush which broke the fall, otherwise I must have met with serious injury. As it was, when I recovered my momentary loss of consciousness, I found that I had sustained no worse harm than a severe shaking, scratches galore, and the utter demolition of my clothes! I picked myself up with difficulty, and spent some time searching for my hat and stick--which I at length discovered, lodged, of course, where one would least have thought of looking for them. I then took close stock of my surroundings, and found them even grimmer than I had anticipated. Though the trees were packed closely together, and there was much undergrowth, the moonbeams were so powerful and so fully concentrated on the spinney, that I could see no inconsiderable distance ahead of me. Over everything hung a solemn and preternatural hush. I saw shadows everywhere--shadows that defied analysis and had no material counterparts. A sudden crashing of brushwood brought me to a standstill, and sent the blood in columns to my heart. Then I laughed loudly--it was only a hare, the prettiest and pertest thing imaginable. I went on. Something whizzed past my face. I drew back in horror--it was a bat, merely a bat. My nerves were out of order, the fall had unsteadied them; I must pull myself together. I did so, and continued to advance. A shadow, long, narrow, and grotesque, fell across my path, and sent a thousand and one icy shivers down my back. In an agony of terror I shut my eyes and plunged madly on. Something struck me in the face and hurled me back. My eyes opened involuntarily, and I saw a tree that, either out of pique or sheer obstinacy, had planted itself half-way across the path. I examined its branches to make sure they _were_ branches, and continued my march. A score more paces, a sudden bend, and I was in an open space, brilliantly illuminated by moonbeams and peopled with countless, moving shadows. One would have to go far to find a wilder, weirder, and more grimly suggestive spot. As I stood gazing at the scene in awestruck wonder, a slight breeze rocked the tops of the pine trees, and moaning through their long and gloomy aisles reverberated like thunder. The sounds, suggesting slightly, ever so slightly, a tattoo, brought with them vivid pictures of the Drummer, too vivid just then to be pleasant, and I turned to go. To my unmitigated horror, a white and lurid object barred my way. My heart ceased to beat, my blood turned to ice; I was sick, absolutely sick, with terror. Besides this, the figure held me spellbound--I could neither move nor utter a sound. It had a white, absolutely white face, a tall, thin, perpendicular frame, and a small, glittering, rotund head. For some seconds it remained stationary, and then, with a gliding motion, left the path and vanished in the shadows.

Again a breeze rustled through the tops of the pine trees, moaned through their long and gloomy aisles, and reverberated like thunder; rat-tat, tat, rat-tat, tat--and with this sound beating in my ears, reaction set in, and I never ceased running till I had reached my hotel.

CASE IX

THE ROOM BEYOND. AN ACCOUNT OF THE
HAUNTINGS AT HENNERSLEY, NEAR AYR

To me Hennersley is what the Transformation Scene at a Pantomime was to the imaginative child--the dreamy child of long ago--a floral paradise full of the most delightful surprises. Here, at Hennersley, from out the quite recently ice-bound earth, softened and moistened now by spring rain, there rises up row upon row of snowdrops, hyacinths and lilies, of such surpassing sweetness and beauty that I hold my breath in astonishment, and ecstatically chant a Te Deum to the fairies for sending such white-clad loveliness.

And then--then, ere my wonder has had time to fade, it is summer. The ground opens, and there springs up, on all sides, a veritable sea of vivid, variegated colour,--scarlet, pink, and white geraniums; red, white and yellow roses; golden honeysuckle; bright-hued marigolds; purple pansies; pale forget-me-nots; wallflowers; sweet peas; many-tinted azaleas; showy hydrangeas; giant rhododendrons; foxgloves, buttercups, daisies, hollyhocks, and heliotropes; a floral host too varied to enumerate.

Overcome with admiration, bewildered with happiness, I kneel on the soft carpet of grass, and, burying my face extravagantly, in alternate laps of luxurious, downy, scent-laden petals, fill my lungs with soul-inspiring nectar.

My intoxication has barely worn off before my eyes are dimly conscious that the soil all around me is generously besprinkled with the remains of my floral friends. I spring hurriedly to my feet, and, gazing anxiously about me, suddenly perceive the gaily nodding heads of new arrivals--dahlias, sunflowers, anemones, chrysanthemums. As I continue gazing, the aromatic odour of mellow apples from the Hennersley orchards reaches my nostrils; I turn round, and there, there in front of me, I see row upon row of richly-laden fruit trees, their leaves a brilliant copper in the scintillating rays of the ruddy autumn sun. I gasp for breath--the beauty of tint and tone surpasses all that I have hitherto seen--it is sublime, the grand climax of transformation. As the curtain falls with the approach of winter, I hurry to my Edinburgh home and pray for the prompt return of early spring.

For many years my aged relatives, the Misses Amelia and Deborah Harbordeens, lived at Hennersley. Rarest and kindest of old ladies, they were the human prototypes of the flowers both they and I loved. Miss Amelia, with her beautiful complexion, rounded form and regal mien, suggested to my childish mind more, much more, than the mere semblance of a rose, whilst Miss Deborah, with her sprightly grace and golden hair, was only masquerading as a woman--she was in reality a daffodil.

Unlike so many of the fair sex who go in for gardening, my aunts were essentially dainty. Their figures were shapely and elegant, their hands slim and soft. I never saw them working without gloves, and I have good reason to believe they anointed their fingers every night with a special preparation to keep them smooth and white. They were not--decidedly not--"brainy," neither were they accomplished, never having made any special study of the higher arts; but they evinced nevertheless the keenest appreciation of painting, music, and literature. Their library--a large one--boasted a delightful harbourage of such writers as Jane Austen, Miss Mitford, and Maria Edgeworth. And in their drawing-room, on the walls of which art was represented by the old as well as modern masters, might be seen and sometimes heard--for the Misses Harbordeens often entertained--a well-tuned Broadwood, and a Bucksen harpsichord. I will describe this old-world abode, not as I first saw it, for when I first visited my aunts Amelia and Deborah, I was only one year old, but as I first remember it--a house with the glamour of a many-gabled roof and diamond window-panes.

The house stood by the side of the turnpike road--that broad, white, interminable road, originating from goodness knows where in the north, and passing through Ayr--the nearest town of any importance--to goodness knows where in the south. A shady avenue, entered by a wooden swing gate bearing the superscription "Hennersley" in neat, white letters, led by a circuitous route to it, and not a vestige of it could be seen from the road. In front of it stretched a spacious lawn, flanked on either side and at the farthest extremity by a thick growth of chestnuts, beeches, poplars, and evergreens.

The house itself was curiously built. It consisted of two storeys, and formed a main building and one wing, which gave it a peculiarly lop-sided appearance that reminded me somewhat ludicrously of Chanticleer, with a solitary, scant, and clipped appendage.

It was often on the tip of my tongue to ask my relatives the reason of this singular disparity; whether it was the result of a mere whim on the part of the architect, or whether it had been caused by some catastrophe; but my curiosity was always held in check by a strange feeling that my relatives would not like to be approached on the subject. My aunts Amelia and Deborah belonged to that class of people, unhappily rare, who possess a power of generating in others an instinctive knowledge of "dangerous ground"--a power which enabled them to avert, both from themselves and the might-be offender, many a painful situation. To proceed--the nakedness of the walls of Hennersley was veiled--who shall say it was not designedly veiled--by a thick covering of clematis and ivy, and in the latter innumerable specimens of the feathered tribe found a sure and safe retreat.

On entering the house, one stepped at once into a large hall. A gallery ran round it, and from the centre rose a broad oak staircase. The rooms, with one or two exceptions, opened into one another, and were large, and low and long in shape; the walls and floors were of oak and the ceilings were crossed by ponderous oak beams.

The fireplaces, too, were of the oldest fashion; and in their comfortable ingle-nook my aunts--in the winter--loved to read or knit.

When the warm weather came, they made similar use of the deep-set window-sills, over which they indulgently permitted me to scramble on to the lawn.

The sunlight was a special feature of Hennersley. Forcing its way through the trellised panes, it illuminated the house with a radiancy, a soft golden radiancy I have never seen elsewhere.

My relatives seemed to possess some phenomenal attraction for the sunlight, for, no matter where they sat, a beam brighter than the rest always shone on them; and, when they got up, I noticed that it always followed them, accompanying them from room to room and along the corridors.

But this was only one of the many pleasant mysteries that added to the joy of my visits to Hennersley. I felt sure that the house was enchanted--that it was under the control of some benevolent being who took a kindly interest in the welfare of my relatives.

I remember once, on the occasion of my customary good-morning to Miss Amelia, who invariably breakfasted in bed, I inhaled the most delicious odour of heliotrope. It was wafted towards me, in a cool current of air, as I approached her bed, and seemed, to my childish fancy, to be the friendly greeting of a sparkling sunbeam that rested on Miss Amelia's pillow.

I was so charmed with the scent, that, alas! forgetful of my manners, I gave a loud sniff, and with a rapturous smile ejaculated, "Oh! Auntie! Cherry pie!"

Miss Amelia started. "Dear me, child!" she exclaimed, "how quietly you entered. I had no idea you were in the room. Heliotrope is the name of the scent, my dear, but please do not allude to it again. Your Aunt Deborah and I are very fond of it"--here she sighed-- "but for certain reasons--reasons you would not understand--we do not like to hear the word heliotrope mentioned. Kiss me, dear, and run away to your breakfast."

For the first time in my life, perhaps, I was greatly puzzled. I could not see why I should be forbidden to refer to such a pleasant and harmless subject--a subject that, looked at from no matter what point of view, did not appear to me to be in the slightest degree indelicate. The more I thought over it, the more convinced I became that there was some association between the scent and the sunbeam, and in that association I felt sure much of the mystery lay.

The house was haunted--agreeably, delightfully haunted by a golden light, a perfumed radiant light that could only have in my mind one origin, one creator--Titania--Titania, queen of the fairies, the guardian angel of my aged, my extremely aged relatives.

"Aunt Deborah," I said one morning, as I found her seated in the embrasure of the breakfast room window crocheting, "Aunt Deborah! You love the sunlight, do you not?"

She turned on me a startled face. "What makes you ask such strange questions, child?" she said. "Of course I like the--sun. Most people do. It is no uncommon thing, especially at my age."

"But the sunbeams do not follow every one, auntie, do they?" I persisted.

Miss Deborah's crochet fell into her lap.

"How queerly you talk," she said, with a curious trembling of her lips. "How can the sunbeams follow one?"

"But they do, auntie, they do indeed!" I cried. "I have often watched a bright beam of golden light follow Aunt Amelia and you, in different parts of the room. And it has settled on your lace collar now."

Miss Deborah looked at me very seriously; but the moistening of her eyes I attributed to the strong light. "Esther," she said, laying one of her soft hands on my forehead, "there are things God does not want little girls to understand--question me no more."

I obeyed, but henceforth I felt more than ever assured that my aunts, consciously or unconsciously, shared their charming abode with some capricious genii, of whose presence in their midst I had become accidentally aware; and to find out the enchanted neighbourhood of its mysterious retreat was to me now a matter of all-absorbing importance. I spent hour after hour roaming through the corridors, the copses, and my beloved flower gardens, in eager search of some spot I could unhesitatingly affirm was the home of the genii. Most ardently I then hoped that the sunbeams would follow me, and that the breeze charged with cool heliotrope would greet me as it did Aunt Deborah.

In the daytime, all Hennersley was sunshine and flowers, and, stray where I would, I never felt lonely or afraid; but as the light waned I saw and felt a subtle change creep over everything. The long aisles of trees that in the morning only struck me as enchantingly peaceful and shady, gradually filled with strangely terrifying shadows; the hue of the broad swards deepened into a darkness I did not dare interpret, whilst in the house, in its every passage, nook, and corner, a gloom arose that, seeming to come from the very bowels of the earth, brought with it every possible suggestion of bogey.

I never spoke of these things to my relatives, partly because I was ashamed of my cowardice, and partly because I dreaded a fresh rebuke. How I suffered! and how I ridiculed my sufferings in the mornings, when every trace of darkness was obliterated, and amid the radiant bloom of the trees I thought only of heliotrope and sunbeams.

One afternoon my search for the abode of the genii led me to the wingless side of the house, a side I rarely visited. At the foot of the ivy-covered walls and straight in their centre was laid a wide bed of flowers, every one of which was white. But why white? Again and again I asked myself this question, but I dared not broach it to my relatives. A garden all white was assuredly an enigma--and to every enigma there is undoubtedly a key. Was this garden, which was all white, in any way connected with the sunbeams and heliotrope? Was it another of the mysteries God concealed from little girls? Could this be the home of the genii? This latter idea had no sooner entered my head than it became a conviction. Of course! There was no doubt whatever--it was the home of the genii.

The white petals were now a source of peculiar interest to me. I was fascinated: the minutes sped by and still I was there. It was not until the sun had disappeared in the far-distant horizon, and the grim shadows of twilight were creeping out upon me from the neighbouring trees and bushes, that I awoke from my reverie--and fled!

That night--unable to sleep through the excitement caused by my discovery of the home of the genii--I lay awake, my whole thoughts concentrated in one soul-absorbing desire, the passionate desire to see the fairy of Hennersley--I had never heard of ghosts--and hear its story. My bedroom was half-way down the corridor leading from the head of the main staircase to the extremity of the wing.

After I said good-night I did not see my aunts again till the morning--they never by any chance visited me after I was in bed. Hence I knew, when I had retired for the night, I should not see a human face nor hear a human voice for nearly twelve hours. This--when I thought of the genii with its golden beams of light and scent of heliotrope--did not trouble me; it was only when my thoughts would not run in this channel that I felt any fear, and that fear was not of the darkness itself, but of what the darkness suggested.

On this particular night, for the first few hours, I was sublimely happy, and then a strange restlessness seized me. I was obsessed with a wish to see the flower-garden. For some minutes, stimulated by a dread of what my aunts would think of such a violation of conventionality on the part of a child, I combated furiously with the desire; but at length the longing was so great, so utterly and wholly irresistible, that I succumbed, and, getting quietly out of bed, made my way noiselessly into the corridor.

All was dark and still--stiller than I had ever known it before. Without any hesitation I plunged forward, in the direction of the wingless side of the house, where there was a long, narrow, stained window that commanded an immediate prospect of the white garden.

I had seldom looked out of it, as up to the present this side of the house had little attraction for me; but all was changed now; and, as I felt my way cautiously along the corridor, a thousand and one fanciful notions of what I might see surged through my brain.

I came to the end of the corridor, I descended half a dozen stairs, I got to the middle of the gallery overlooking the large entrance hall--below me, above me, on all sides of me, was Stygian darkness. I stopped, and there suddenly rang out, apparently from close at hand, a loud, clear, most appallingly clear, blood-curdling cry, which, beginning in a low key, ended in a shriek so horrid, harsh, and piercing, that I felt my heart shrivel up within me, and in sheer desperation I buried my fingers in my ears to deaden the sound.

I was now too frightened to move one way or the other. All the strength departed from my limbs, and when I endeavoured to move my feet, I could not-- they appeared to be fastened to the ground with lead weights.

I felt, I intuitively felt that the author of the disturbance was regarding my terror with grim satisfaction, and that it was merely postponing further action in order to enjoy my suspense. To block out the sight of this dreadful creature, I clenched my eyelids tightly together, at the same time earnestly imploring God to help me.

Suddenly I heard the low wail begin again, and then the echo of a far-off silvery voice came softly to me through the gloom: "It's an owl--only an owl!"

With lightning-like rapidity the truth then dawned on me, and as I withdrew my clammy finger-tips from my ears, the faint fluttering of wings reached me, through an open skylight. Once again I moved on; the gallery was left behind, and I was well on my way down the tortuous passage leading to my goal, when a luminous object, of vast height and cylindrical shape, suddenly barred my progress.

Overcome by a deadly sickness, I sank on the floor, and, burying my face in my hands, quite made up my mind that my last moments had come.

How long I remained in this position I cannot say, to me it seemed eternity. I was eventually freed from it by the echo of a gentle laugh, so kind, and gay, and girlish, that my terror at once departed, and, on raising my head, I perceived that the cause of my panic was nothing more than a broad beam of moonlight on a particularly prominent angle of the wall.

Heartily ashamed at my cowardice, I got up, and, stepping briskly forward, soon reached the stained-glass window.

Pressing my face against the pane, I peered through it, and there immediately beneath me lay the flowers, glorified into dazzling gold by the yellow colour of the glass. The sight thrilled me with joy--it was sublime. My instinct had not deceived me, this was indeed the long-looked-for home of the genii.

The temperature, which had been high, abnormally so for June, now underwent an abrupt change, and a chill current of air, sweeping down on me from the rear, made my teeth chatter. I involuntarily shrank back from the window, and, as I did so, to my utter astonishment it disappeared, and I saw, in its place, a room.

It was a long, low room, and opposite to me, at the farthest extremity, was a large bay window, through which I could see the nodding tops of the trees. The furniture was all green and of a lighter, daintier make than any I had hitherto seen. The walls were covered with pictures, the mantelshelf with flowers. Whilst I was busily employed noting all these details, the door of the room opened, and the threshold was gorgeously illuminated by a brilliant sunbeam, from which suddenly evolved the figure of a young and lovely girl.

I can see her now as I saw her then--tall, and slender, with masses of golden hair, waved artistically aside from a low forehead of snowy white; finely-pencilled brows, and long eyes of the most lustrous violet; a straight, delicately-moulded nose, a firm, beautifully-proportioned chin, and a bewitching mouth. At her bosom was a bunch of heliotrope, which, deftly undoing, she raised to her nose and then laughingly held out to me. I was charmed; I took a step forward towards her. The instant I did so, a wild look of terror distorted her face, she waved me back, something jarred against my knee, and, in the place of the room,

I saw only the blurred outline of trees through the yellow window-panes.

Bitterly disappointed, but absolutely sure that what I had seen was objective, I retraced my steps to my bedroom and passed the remainder of the night in sound sleep.

After breakfast, however, unable to restrain my curiosity longer, I sought Miss Amelia, who was easier to approach than her sister, and, managing after several efforts to screw up courage, blurted out the story of my nocturnal escapade.

My aunt listened in silence. She was always gentle, but on this occasion she surpassed herself.

"I am not going to scold you, Esther," she said, smoothing out my curls. "After what you have seen it is useless to conceal the truth from you. God perhaps intends you to know all. Years ago, Esther, this house was not as you see it now. It had two wings, and, in the one that no longer exists was the bedroom you saw in your vision. We called it the Green Room because everything in it was green, your Aunt Alicia-- an aunt you have never heard of--who slept there, having a peculiar fancy for that colour.

"Alicia was our youngest sister, and we all loved her dearly. She was just as you describe her--beautiful as a fairy, with golden hair, and violet eyes, and she always wore a bunch of heliotrope in her dress.

98

"One night, Esther, one lovely, calm, midsummer night, forty years ago, this house was broken into by burglars. They got in through the Green Room window, which was always left open during the warm weather. We--my mother, your Aunt Deborah, and I-- were awakened by a loud shriek for help. Recognising Alicia's voice, we instantly flew out of bed, and, summoning the servants, tore to the Green Room as fast as we could.

"To our horror, Esther, the door was locked, and before we could break the lock the ruffians had murdered her! They escaped through the window and were never caught. My mother, your great-grandmother, had that part of the house pulled down, and on the site of it she planted the white garden.

"Though Alicia's earthly body died, and was taken from us, her beautiful spirit remains with us here. It follows us about in the daytime in the form of a sunbeam, whilst occasionally, at night, it assumes her earthly shape. The house is what is generally termed haunted, and, no doubt, some people would be afraid to live in it. But that, Esther, is because they do not understand spirits--your Aunt Deborah and I do."

"Do you think, auntie," I asked with a thrill of joy, "do you think it at all likely that I shall see Aunt Alicia again to-night?"

Aunt Amelia shook her head gently. "No, my dear," she said slowly, "I think it will be impossible, because you are going home this afternoon."

CASE X

"---- HOUSE," NEAR BLYTHSWOOD SQUARE, GLASGOW. THE HAUNTED BATH

When Captain W. de S. Smythe went to look over "----
House," in the neighbourhood of Blythswood Square,
Glasgow, the only thing about the house he did not
like was the bathroom--it struck him as excessively
grim. The secret of the grimness did not lie, he
thought, in any one particular feature--in the tall,
gaunt geyser, for example (though there was always
something in the look of a geyser when it was old and
dilapidated, as was the case with this one, that
repelled him), or in the dark drying-cupboard, or in
the narrow, slit-like window; but in the room as a
whole, in its atmosphere and general appearance. He
could not diagnose it; he could not associate it with
anything else he had ever experienced; it was a
grimness that he could only specify as grim--grim
with a grimness that made him feel he should not like
to be alone there in the dead of night. It was a
nuisance, because the rest of the house pleased him;
moreover, the locality was convenient, and the rent
moderate, very moderate for such a neighbourhood.
He thought the matter well over as he leaned in the

doorway of the bathroom. He could, of course, have the room completely renovated--new paper, new paint, and a fresh bath. Hot-water pipes! The geyser should be done away with. Geysers were hideous, dangerous, and--pshaw, what nonsense!--Ghostly! Ghostly! What absurd rot! How his wife would laugh! That decided the question. His wife! She had expressed a very ardent wish that he should take a house in or near Blythswood Square, if he could get one on anything like reasonable terms, and here was his chance. He would accompany the agent of the property to the latter's office, and the preliminaries should be forthwith settled.

Six weeks later, he and his family were installed in the house, which still reeked with the smell of fresh paint and paper. The first thing the Captain did when he got there was to steal away slyly to the bathroom, and as soon as he opened the door his heart sank. Despite the many alterations the room had undergone, the grimness was still there--there, everywhere. In the fine new six-foot bath, with its glistening, gleaming, wooden framework; in the newly papered, newly painted cupboard; in the walls, with their bright, fresh paper; in the snowy surface of the whitewashed ceiling; in the air,--the very air itself was full of it. The Captain was, as a rule, very fond of his bath, but in his new quarters he firmly resolved that some one else should use the bath before he made the experiment. In a very few days the family had all settled down, and every one, with the exception of the Captain, had had a bath, but no matter how many and how bitter were his wife's complaints, try how he would, he could not, he positively _could_ not, bring himself to wash in the bathroom--_alone_. It was all right so long as the door was open, but his wife resolutely refused to allow him to keep it open, and the moment it was shut his abject terror returned--a terror produced by nothing that he could in any way analyse or define. At last, ashamed of his cowardice, he screwed up courage, and, with a look of determined desperation in his eyes and mouth--an expression which sent his wife into fits of laughter--set out one night from his bedroom, candle in hand, and entered the bathroom. Shutting and locking the door, he lighted another candle, and, after placing them both on the mantelshelf, turned on the bath water, and began to undress.

"I may as well have a peep in the cupboard," he said, "just to satisfy myself no one is hiding there--for every one in the house knows how I hate this beastly bathroom--with the intention of playing me a practical joke. Supposing one of the maids--Polly, for example, I'm sure she'd be quite capable--took it into her pretty head to"--but here the Captain was obliged to stop; he really was not equal to facing, even in his mind's eye, the situation such a supposition involved, and at the bare idea of such a thing his countenance assumed a deeper hue, and--I am loth to admit--an amused grin. The grin, however, died out as he cautiously opened the door and peered furtively in; no one--nothing was there! With a breath of relief he closed the door again, placed a chair against it, and, sitting down, proceeded to pull off his clothes. Coat, vest, under-garments, he placed them all tenderly in an untidy heap on the floor, and then, with a last lingering, affectionate look at them, walked sedately towards the bath. But this sedateness was only momentary.

The first few steps he walked, but, a noise in the grate startling him, he suddenly assumed an air of the greatest gaiety, and, bowing with mock gallantry to his trousers, he now waltzed coquettishly to the bath. It was grim, horribly grim, and horribly hot too, for, when he felt the temperature with one of his squat, podgy toes, it made him swear quite involuntarily. Turning on the cold water, and slapping his thighs playfully, he felt again. Too hot yet, far too hot even for him! He loved heat. More cold! and he was hoisting one chubby leg to feel again, when, a repetition of the noise in the grate making him swing round, he lost his balance, and descended on the floor with a hard, a very hard, bump. For some seconds he lay still, too sulky and aggrieved even to get up, but, the draught from under the ill-fitting door tickling his bare flesh in the most immodest fashion, he roused himself from this lethargy, and was about to raise himself from the floor, when the lights went out--went out without a moment's warning, and he found himself engulfed in the most funereal darkness.

To say he was startled is to put it very mildly--he was absolutely terror-stricken--far too terror-stricken to think of moving now, and least of all of getting up and groping for the matches. Indeed, when he came to think of it, he had not seen any matches in the room, and he had not brought any with him, his wife had flurried him so much. The moment the candles were extinguished the grimness sensibly increased, and he could feel all around him, thickly amalgamated with the ether, a superphysical presence, at once hostile and horrible. Then, to bring his terror to a climax, there issued from the bath a loud rubbing and splashing, as if some one, some very heavy person, was vigorously washing. The water rose and fell, squished and bubbled as it does when one is lying at full length in it, raising and lowering oneself, kicking and plunging first on one side and then on the other. Whilst, to add to the realism, Captain Smythe distinctly heard gasping and puffing; and the soft, greasy sound of a well-soaped flannel. He could indeed follow every movement of the occupant of the bath as graphically as if he had seen him--from the brisk scrubbing of body and legs to the finicky process of cleaning the ears and toes.

It was whilst the bather was occupied thus that the cupboard door began to open very quietly and stealthily, and Captain de Smythe heard the chair he had so carefully placed against it being gradually propelled across the floor.

Then something, he would have given anything to tell what, came out and began to steal towards him. He tried to crawl out of its way, but could not; his limbs no longer acted conjointly with his brain, and when he opened his mouth to shout at it, his voice withered away in his throat. It came up to him, and directly it touched his naked skin he knew it was a woman--a woman with a much-beflounced silk skirt and silk petticoats--a woman whose person was perfumed with violets (a scent for which the Captain had a particular weakness), and without doubt, loaded with jewellery. Her behaviour did not betray any symptoms of embarrassment when she encountered the Captain lying on the floor, but, planting one icy-cold high-heeled shoe on his chest and the other on his cheek, she stepped on him as if he had been an orthodox cushion or footstool, purposely placed there for her convenience.

A hollow exclamation, which died away in a gasp, issued from the bath, as the woman, with a swift movement of her arms, threw something over it. What followed, the Captain could only surmise, but from the muttered imprecations and splashes in the water, it seemed to him that nothing short of murder was taking place. After a while the noises in the bath grew feebler and feebler, and when they finally ceased, the woman, with a sigh of relief, shook the water from her arms, and, stepping off the Captain, moved towards the fireplace. The spell which had, up to the present, enthralled the unfortunate Captain, was now broken, and, thinking that his ghostly visitor had betaken herself right away, he sat up. He had hardly done so before the darkness was rudely dissipated, and, to his horror, he saw looking at him, from a distance of only a few feet, a white, luminous face, presumably that of a woman.

But what a woman! What a devil!--what a match for the most lurid of any of Satan's male retainers. Yet she was not without beauty--beauty of the richest sensual order; beauty that, had it been flesh and blood, would have sent men mad. Her hair, jet black, wavy, and parted in the centre, was looped over her shell-like ears, which were set unusually low and far back on her head; her nose was of that rare and matchless shape termed Grecian; and her mouth--in form, a triumph of all things heavenly, in expression, a triumph of all things hellish. The magnificent turn of its short upper lip, and the soft voluptuous line of its under lip; its sportive dimples and ripe red colour; its even rows of dazzling, pearly teeth were adorable; but they appealed to the senses, and in no sense or shape to the soul. Her brows, slightly irregular in outline, met over the nose; her eyelashes were of great length, and her eyes--slightly, ever so slightly, obliquely set, and larger than those of living human beings--were black, black as her hair; and the pupils sparkled and shone with the most damnable expression of satanical hatred and glee. The whole thing, the face and the light that emanated from it, was so entirely awful and devilish, that Captain Smythe sat like one turned to stone, and it was not until long after it had vanished that he groped his way to the door, and in Adam's costume, for he dared not stay to put on his clothes, fled down the passage to his bedroom.

From his wife he got little sympathy; her sarcasm was too deep for words, and she merely ordered her husband on no account to breathe a word of his "silliness" before either the children or the servants. The injunction, however, which was naturally carried out to the letter, was futile as a precaution, for, on running into the bathroom one morning when every one else was downstairs, the eldest boy, Ronald, saw, floating in the bath, the body of a hoary-headed old man. It was bloated and purplish blue, and had big, glassy eyes that stared at him in such a hideous, meaningless manner that he uttered a scream of terror and fled. Alarmed at the noise, most of the household ran to see what had happened. Only the Captain remained behind. He knew only too well, and he hid, letting his wife and the servants go upstairs alone. They entered the bathroom--there was nothing in the bath, not even water, but, as they were leaving, they ran into a dark, handsome, evil-eyed woman, clad in the most costly of dresses, and sparkling with jewellery. She glided past them with sly, silent footsteps, and vanished by the cupboard. Cured of scepticism, and throwing dignity to the wind, the Captain's wife raced downstairs, and, bursting into the drawing-room, flung herself on the sofa in hysterics.

Within a week the house was once again empty, and the rumour getting about that it was haunted, the landlord threatened the Smythes with an action for slander of title. But I do not think the case was taken to court, the Smythes agreeing to contradict the report they had originated. Astute inquiries, however, eventually led them to discover that a lady, answering to the description of the ghost they had seen, had once lived at ---- House. Of Spanish descent, she was young, beautiful, and gay; and was married to a man, an extremely wealthy man (people remembered how rich he was after he died), old enough to be her grandfather. They had nothing in common, the husband only wanting to be quiet, the wife to flirt and be admired. Their neighbours often heard them quarrel, and it was declared that the wife possessed the temper of a fiend. The man was eventually found dead in his bath, and there being no indications of violence, it was generally supposed that he had fainted, (his wife having been previously heard to declare that he often had fainting fits), and had thus been accidentally drowned. The beautiful young widow, who inherited all his money, left the house immediately and went abroad, and the neighbours, when questioned by the Smythes as to whether anything had been seen of her since, shook their heads dubiously, but refused to commit themselves.

CASE XI

THE CHOKING GHOST OF "---- HOUSE," NEAR SANDYFORD PLACE, GLASGOW

The last time I was passing through Glasgow, I put up for the night at an hotel near Sandyford Place, and met there an old theatrical acquaintance named Browne, Hely Browne. Not having seen him since I gave up acting, which is now, alas! a good many years, we had much to discuss--touring days, lodgings, managers, crowds, and a dozen other subjects, all included in the vulgar term "shop." We spent the whole of one evening debating thus, in the smoke-room; whilst the following night we went to an entertainment given by that charming reciter and raconteur, Miss Lilian North, who, apart from her talent, which, in my opinion, places her in the first rank of her profession, is the possessor of extraordinary personal attractions, not the least remarkable of which are her hands. Indeed, it was through my attention being called to the latter, that I am indirectly indebted for this story. Miss North has typically psychic hands--exquisitely white and narrow, and her long, tapering fingers and filbert nails (which, by the way, are always trimly manicured) are the most perfect I have ever seen. I was alluding to them, on our way back to the hotel after her performance, when Hely Browne interrupted me.

"Talking about psychic things, O'Donnell," he said, "do you know there is a haunted house near where we are staying? You don't? Very well, then, if I tell you what I know and you write about it, will you promise not to allude to the house by its right number? If you do, there will be the dickens to pay--simply call it '----House,' near Sandyford Place. You promise? Good! Let us take a little stroll before we turn in--I feel I want a breath of fresh air--and I will tell you the experience I once had there. It is exactly two years ago, and I was on tour here in _The Green Bushes_. All the usual theatrical 'diggings' had been snapped up long before I arrived, and, not knowing where else to go, I went to No.--Sandyford Place, which I saw advertised in one of the local papers as a first-class private hotel with very moderate charges. A wild bit of extravagance, eh? But then one does do foolish things sometimes, and, to tell the truth, I wanted a change badly. I had 'digged' for a long time with a fellow called Charlie Grosvenor. Not at all a bad chap, but rather apt to get on one's nerves after a while--and he had got on mine--horribly. Consequently, I was not at all sorry for an excuse to get away from him for a bit, even though I had to pay dearly for it. A private hotel in a neighbourhood like that of Sandyford Place is a big order for an ordinary comedian. I forget exactly what the terms were, but I know I pulled rather a long face when I was told. Still, being, as I say, tired of the usual 'digs,' I determined to try it, and accordingly found myself landed in a nice-sized bedroom on the second floor. The first three nights passed, and nothing happened, saving that I had the most diabolical nightmares--a very unusual thing for me. 'It was the cheese,' I said to myself, when I got out of bed the first morning; 'I will take very good care I don't touch cheese to-night.' I kept this resolution, but I had the nightmare again, and even, if anything, worse than before. Then I fancied it must be cocoa--I was at that time a teetotaller--so I took hot milk instead; but I had nightmare all the same, and my dreams terrified me to such an extent that I did not dare get out of bed in the morning (it was then winter) till it was broad daylight. It was now becoming a serious matter with me. As you know, an actor more than most people needs sleep, and it soon became as much as I could do to maintain my usual standard of acting. On the fourth night, determining to get rest at all costs, I took a stiff glass of hot brandy just before getting into bed. I slept,--I could scarcely help sleeping,--but not for long, for I was rudely awakened from my slumbers by a loud crash. I sat up in bed, thinking the whole house was falling about my ears. The sound was not repeated, and all was profoundly silent. Wondering what on earth the noise could have been, and feeling very thirsty, I got out of bed to get a drink of lime-juice. To my annoyance, however, though I groped about everywhere, knocking an ash tray off the mantelpiece and smashing the lid of the soap-dish, I could find neither the lime-juice nor matches. At length, giving it up as a bad job, I decided to get into bed again. With that end in view, I groped my way through the darkness, steering myself by the furniture, the position of which was, of course, quite familiar to me--at least I imagined it was. Judge, then, of my astonishment when I could not find the bed! At first I regarded it as a huge joke, and laughed--how rich! Ha! ha! ha! Fancy not being able to find one's

111

way back to bed in a room of this dimension! Good enough for _Punch_! Too good, perhaps, now. Ha! ha! ha! But it soon grew past a joke. I had been round the room, completely round the room, twice, and still no bed! I became seriously alarmed! Could I be ill? Was I going mad? But no, my forehead was cool, my pulse normal. For some seconds I stood still, not knowing what else to do; then, to make one more desperate attempt, I stuck straight in front of me-- and--ran into something--something that recoiled and hit me. Thrilled with amazement, I put up my hand to feel what it was, and touched a noose."

"A noose!" I ejaculated, interrupting Hely Browne for the first time since he began.

"Yes, a noose!" he repeated, "suspended in mid-air. As you can imagine, I was greatly astonished, for I knew there had been nothing that I could be now mistaking for a noose in the room overnight. I stretched out my arms to feel to what it was fastened, but, to add to my surprise, the cord terminated in thin air. Then I grew frightened, and, dropping my arms, tried to move away from the spot; I could not--my feet were glued to the floor. With a gentle, purring sound the noose commenced fawning--I use that word because the action was so intensely bestial, so like that of a cat or snake--round my neck and face. It then rose above me, and, after circling furiously round and round and creating a miniature maelstrom in the air, descended gradually over my head. Lower and lower it stole, like some sleek, caressing slug. Now past the tips of my

112

ears, now my nose, now my chin, until with a tiny thud it landed on my shoulders, when, with a fierce snap, it suddenly tightened. I endeavoured to tear it off, but every time I raised my hands, a strong, magnetic force drew them to my side again; I opened my mouth to shriek for help, and an icy current of air froze the breath in my lungs. I was helpless, O'Donnell, utterly, wholly helpless. Cold, clammy hands tore my feet from the floor; I was hoisted bodily up, and then let drop. A frightful pain shot through me. A hundred wires cut into my throat at once. I gasped, choked, suffocated, and in my mad efforts to find a foothold kicked out frantically in all directions. But this only resulted in an increase of my torments, since with every plunge the noose grew tauter. My agony at last grew unbearable; I could feel the sides of my raw and palpitating thorax driven into one another, while every attempt to heave up breath from my bursting lungs was rewarded with the most excruciating paroxysms of pain--pain more acute than I thought it possible for any human being to endure. My head became ten times its natural size; blood--foaming, boiling blood--poured into it from God knows where, and under its pressure my eyes bulged in their sockets, and the veins in my nose cracked. Terrific thunderings echoed and re-echoed in my ears; my tongue, huge as a mountain, shot against my teeth; a sea of fire raged through my brain, and then--blackness--blackness inconceivable. When I recovered consciousness, O'Donnell, I found myself standing, cold and shivering, but otherwise sound and whole, on the chilly oilcloth. I had, now, no difficulty in finding my way back to bed, and in about an hour's time succeeded in falling asleep. I slept till late, and, on getting up, tried to persuade myself that my horrible experience was but the result of another nightmare.

"As you may guess, after all this, I did not look forward to bedtime, and counted the minutes as they flew by with the utmost regret. Never had I been so sorry when my performance at the theatre was over, and the lights of my hotel once again hove in sight. I entered my bedroom in fear and trembling, and was so apprehensive lest I should be again compelled to undergo the sensations of hanging, that I decided to keep a light burning all night, and, for that reason, had bought half a pound of wax candles. At last I grew so sleepy that I could keep awake no longer, and, placing the candlestick on a chair by the bed, I scrambled in between the sheets. Without as much as a sip of spirits, I slept like a top. When I awoke the room was in pitch darkness. A curious smell at once attracted my notice. I thought, at first, it might be but the passing illusion of a dream. But no--I sniffed again--it was there--there, close to me--under my very nose--the strong, pungent odour of drugs; but not being a professor of smells, nor even a humble student of physics, I was consequently unable to diagnose it, and could only arrive at the general conclusion that it was a smell that brought with it very vivid recollections of a chemist's shop and of my old school laboratory. Wondering whence it originated, I thrust my face forward with the intention of trying to locate it, when, to my horror, my lips touched against something cold and flabby. In an agony of fear I reeled away from it, and, the bed being narrow, I slipped over the edge and bumped on to the floor.

"Now I think it is quite possible that up to this point you may have attributed my unhappy experience to nothing more nor less than a bad dream, but your dream theory can no longer hold good, for, on coming in such sudden contact with the floor, I gave my funny-bone a knock, which, I can assure you, made me thoroughly awake, and the first thing I noticed on recovering my scattered senses--was the smell. I sat up, and saw to my terror my bed was occupied, but occupied in the most alarming manner. On the middle of the pillow was a face, the face of--I looked closer; I would have given every penny I possessed not to have done so, but I could not help myself--I looked closer, and it was--the face of my brother; my brother Ralph--you may recollect my mentioning him to you, for he was the only one of us who was at that time making money--whom I believed to be in New York. He had always been rather sallow, but apart from the fact that he now looked very yellow, his appearance was quite natural. Indeed, as I gazed at him, I grew so convinced it was he that I cried out, 'Ralph!' The moment I did so, there was a ghastly change: his eyelids opened, and his eyes--eyes I recognised at once--protruded to such a degree that they almost rolled out; his mouth flew open, his tongue swelled, his whole countenance became convulsed with the most unparalleled, and for that reason indescribable, expression of agony, whilst the yellowness of his complexion deepened to a livid, lurid black, that was so inconceivably repellent and hellish that I sprang away from the bed--appalled. There was then a gasping, rasping noise, and a voice that, despite its unnatural hollowness, I identified as that of Ralph, broke forth: 'I have been wanting to speak to you for ages, but _something_, I cannot explain, has always prevented me. I have been dead a month; not cancer, but Dolly. Poison. Good-bye, Hely. I shall rest in peace now.' The voice stopped; there was a rush of cold air, laden with the scent of the drug, and tainted, faintly tainted, with the nauseating smell of the grave, and--the face on the pillow vanished. How I got through the remainder of the night I cannot say--I dare not think. I dare only remember that I did not sleep. I was devoted to Ralph, and the thought that he had perished in the miserable manner suggested by the apparition, completely prostrated me. In the morning I received a black-edged letter from my mother, stating that she had just heard from Dolly, my brother's wife, saying Ralph had died from cancer in the throat. Dolly added in a postscript that her dearly beloved Ralph had been very good to her, and left her well provided for. Of course, we might have had the body exhumed, but we were poor, and Ralph's widow was rich; and in America, you know, everything goes in favour of the dollars. Hence we were obliged to let the matter drop, sincerely trusting Dolly would never take it into her head to visit us. She never did. My mother died last year--I felt her death terribly, O'Donnell; and as I no longer have any fixed abode, but am always touring the British provinces, there is not much fear of Ralph's murderess and I meeting. It is rather odd, however, that after my own experience at the hotel, I heard that it had borne the reputation for being haunted for many years, and that a good many visitors who had passed the night in one of the rooms (presumably mine) had complained of hearing strange noises and having dreadful dreams. How can one explain it all?"

"One can't," I responded, as we turned in for the night.

CASE XII

THE GREY PIPER AND THE HEAVY COACH OF DONALDGOWERIE HOUSE, PERTH

Donaldgowerie House, until comparatively recent times, stood on the outskirts of Perth. It was a long, low, rambling old place, dating back to the beginning of the seventeenth century. At the time of the narrative it was in the possession of a Mr. William Whittingen, who bought it at a very low price from some people named Tyler. It is true that it would cost a small fortune to repair, but, notwithstanding this disadvantage, Mr. Whittingen considered his purchase a bargain, and was more than satisfied with it. Indeed, he knew of no other house of a similar size, of such an imposing appearance, and so pleasantly situated, that he could have bought for less than twice the amount he had paid for this; and he was really very sorry for the Tylers, who explained to him, in confidence, that had they not been in such urgent need of money, they would never have sold Donaldgowerie House at such a ridiculously low figure. However, with them it was a question of cash-- cash down, and Mr. Whittingen had only to write out a cheque for the modest sum they asked, and the house was his. It was June when Mr. Whittingen took possession of the house--June, when the summer sun was brightest and the gardens looked their best. The Whittingen family, consisting of Mr. and Mrs. Whittingen, two sons, Ernest and Harvey, and three daughters, Ruth, Martha, and Mary, were, as one might gather from their names alone, plain, practical, genteel, and in fact very superior people, who were by no means lacking in that exceedingly useful quality of canniness, so characteristic of the Lowland Scot to which race they belonged. Mr. Whittingen had, for years, conducted a grocery business in Jedburgh, twice filling the honoured and coveted post of mayor, and when he at length retired into private life, his friends (and it was astonishing how many friends he had) shrewdly suspected that his pockets were not only well lined but full to bursting. Acting on the advice of his wife and daughters, who were keen on social distinction, he sent Ernest to Oxford, conditionally that he should take Holy Orders in the Church of England, whilst Harvey, who, when scarcely out of the petticoat stage, displayed the regular Whittingen talent for business by covertly helping himself to the sugar in his father's shop, and disposing of it at strictly sale price to his sisters' cronies in the nursery, was sent to one of those half preparatory and half finishing schools (of course, for the sons of gentlemen only) at Edinburgh, where he was kept till he was old enough to be articled to a prosperous, exceedingly prosperous, firm of solicitors.

The girls, Ruth, Martha, and Mary, had likewise been highly educated, that is to say, they had remained so many years at an English seminary for young ladies, and had been given a final twelve months in France and Germany to enable them to obtain "the correct accent."

At the time of the story they were as yet unmarried, and were awaiting with the most laudable patience the advent of men of title. They were delighted with their new home (which Ruth had persuaded her father to christen "Donaldgowerie," after the house in a romantic novel she had just been reading), and proud of their gilded premises and magnificent tennis lawns; they had placed a gigantic and costly tray in the hall, in confident assurance that it would speedily groan beneath the weight of cards from all the gentry in Perthshire.

But please be it understood, that my one and only object in alluding to these trifling details is to point out that the Whittingens, being entirely engrossed in matters mundane, were the very last people in the world to be termed superstitious, and although imaginative where future husbands' calls and cards were concerned, prior to the events about to be narrated had not an ounce of superstition in their natures. Indeed, until then they had always smiled in a very supercilious manner at even the smallest mention of a ghost.

September came, their first September in Donaldgowerie, and the family welcomed with joy Ernest and his youthful bride.

The latter was not, as they had fondly hoped (and roundly announced in Perth), the daughter of a Peer, but of a wealthy Bristol draper, the owner of a house near the Downs, whose son had been one of Ernest's many friends at Oxford. The coming of the newly-married pair to Donaldgowerie brought with it a burst of bird-like gaiety. All sorts of entertainments-- musical "at homes," dinners, dances, tennis and garden parties, in fact, every variety that accorded with the family's idea of good taste--were given; and with praiseworthy "push," for which the Whittingens had fast become noted, all the County was invited. This splendid display of wealth and hospitality was not disinterested; I fear, it might be not only accounted a "send off" for the immaculately-clad curate and his wife, but also a determined effort on the part of Mr. and Mrs. Whittingen to attract the right sort of lover for their girls. It was during the progress of one of their alfresco entertainments that the scepticism of certain of the Whittingens with regard to the supernatural received a rude blow. Martha, Mary, and two eligible young men, friends of Harvey's, having finished a somewhat spirited game of croquet, were refreshing themselves with lemonade, whilst they continued their flirtation.

Presently Mary, whose partner declared how much he should like to see some photographs she had recently had taken of herself, with a well-affected giggle of embarrassment set off to the house to fetch her album. The minutes passed, and, as she did not return, Martha went in search of her. The album, she knew, was in their boudoir, which was situated at the end of the long and rather gloomy corridor of the upper storey. Highly incensed at her sister's slowness, she was hastening along the corridor, when, to her supreme astonishment, she suddenly saw the figure of a man in kilts, with a bagpipe under his arm, emerge through the half-open door of the boudoir, and with a peculiar gliding motion advance towards her. A curious feeling, with which she was totally unfamiliar, compelled her to remain mute and motionless; and in this condition she awaited the approach of the stranger. Who was he? she asked herself, and how on earth had he got there, and what was he doing? As he drew nearer, she perceived that his face was all one hue,--a ghastly, livid grey,--and that his eyes, which were all the time fixed on hers, were lurid and menacing,--so terrible, in fact, that she turned cold with fear, and felt the very hair on her head beginning to rise on end. She opened her mouth to shriek, but found she could not ejaculate a syllable; neither could she, even with the most desperate efforts, tear her feet from the floor. On came the figure, and, without swerving either to the right or left, it glided right up to and through her; and, as she involuntarily turned round, she saw it disappear through a half-open staircase window, at least twenty feet above the ground outside.

Shaking all over with terror, and not understanding in the slightest what to make of it, Martha ran to the boudoir, where her heart almost sprang out of her body at the spectacle of her sister Mary stretched at full length on the floor, her cheeks ashy pale, her lips blue. Martha at once made a frantic rush to the bell, and, in a few minutes, half the establishment, headed by Mr. Whittingen, poured into the room. With the aid of a little cold water, Mary speedily recovered, and, in reply to the anxious inquiries of her sympathetic rescuers as to what had happened, indignantly demanded why such a horrible looking creature as "that" piper had been allowed not merely to enter the house but to come up to her room, and half frighten her to death. "I had just got my album," she added, "when, feeling some one was in the room, I turned round--and there (she indicated a spot on the carpet) was the piper, not ten paces away from me, regarding me with the most awful look imaginable. I was too taken aback with surprise to say anything, nor--for some unaccountable reason--could I escape, before he touched me on the shoulder with one of his icy cold hands, and then commenced playing. Up and down the floor he paced, backwards and forwards, never taking his hateful glance off my face and ever piping the same dismal dirge. At last, unable to stand the strain of it any longer, and convinced he was a madman, bent on murdering me--for who but a lunatic would behave in such a way?--I gave way to a violent fit of hysterics, and fainted. Now tell me who he was, and why he was permitted to frighten me in this manner?" And Mary stamped her feet and grew vicious, as only her class will when they are at all vexed. Her speech was followed by a silence that exasperated her. She repeated her inquiries with crimson cheeks, and then, as again no one responded, she signalled out the head footman and raved at him. Up to this point Mr. Whittingen had been dumb with amazement. The idea of a strange piper having the twofold effrontery to enter his house and proceed to the private and chaste sanctuary of his highly respectable daughters, almost deprived him of breath. He could scarcely believe his ears. "What--what in the name of--what does it all mean?" he at length stammered, addressing the unfortunate footman. "A piper! and without any invitation from me, how dare you let him in?"

"I did not, sir," the luckless footman replied; "no such person came to the door when I was in the hall."

"No more he did when I was there," chimed in the second footman, and all the other servants vociferated in a body, "We never saw any piper, sir, nor heard one either," and they looked at Mary reproachfully.

At this Mr. Whittingen looked exceedingly embarrassed. In the face of such a unanimous denial what could he say? He knew if he suggested the servants were untruthful they would all give notice to leave on the spot, and knowing good servants are scarce in Perth as elsewhere, he felt rather in a fix. At length, turning to Mary, he asked if she was sure it was a piper. "Sure!" Mary screamed, "why, of course I am, did I not tell you he marched up and down here playing on his disgusting bagpipes, which nearly broke the drum of my ear."

"And I saw him too, pa," Martha put in. "I met him in the corridor, he had his pipes under his arm, and the most dreadful expression in his face. I don't wonder Mary was frightened."

"But where did he go?" Mr. Whittingen cried.

"You would not believe me if I told you," Martha said, her cheeks flushing. "He seemed to pass right through me, and then to vanish through the staircase window. I have never been so terribly upset in my life," and, sinking on to the sofa, she began to laugh hysterically.

"Dear me! dear me! it is very odd!" Mr. Whittingen exclaimed, as Mary handed her sister a wineglass of sal-volatile. "They can't both have been dreaming; it must--but there, what a nonsensical notion, there are no such things as ghosts! Only children and nursemaids believe in them nowadays. As soon as you have quite recovered, my dears, we will return to the garden, and I think that under the circumstances, the rather peculiar circumstances, ahem! it will be better to say nothing to your mother. Do you understand?" Mr. Whittingen went on, eyeing the servants, "Nothing to your mistress."

The affair thus terminated, and for some days nothing further happened to disturb the peace of the family. At the end of a week, however, exactly a week after the appearance of the piper, Mary met with a serious accident. She was running across the croquet lawn to speak to her sister-in-law, when she tripped over a hoop that had been accidentally left there, and, in falling, ran a hatpin into her head. Blood poisoning ensued, and within a fortnight she was dead. Martha was the only one in the house, however, who associated Mary's accident and death with the piper; to her that sinister expression in the mysterious Highlander's eyes portended mischief, and she could not but suspect that, in some way or another, he had brought about the catastrophe. The autumn waned, and Christmas was well within sight, when another mysterious occurrence took place. It was early one Sunday evening, tea was just over, and the Whittingen family were sitting round the fire engaged in a somewhat melancholy conversation, for the loss of Mary had affected them all very deeply, when they heard the far-away rumble of a heavy coach on the high-road. Nearer and nearer it came, till it seemed to be about on a level with the front lodge gate; then to their surprise there was a loud crunching of gravel, and they heard it careering at a breakneck speed up the carriage-drive. They looked at one another in the utmost consternation.

"A coach, and driven in this mad fashion! Whose was it? What did it mean? Not visitors, surely!"

It pulled up at the front door, and the champing and stamping of the horses vibrated loudly through the still night air. Sounds as of one or more people descending were next heard, and then there came a series of the most terrific knockings at the door. The Whittingen family stared at one another aghast; there was something in those knockings--something they could not explain--that struck terror in their souls and made their blood run cold. They waited in breathless anxiety for the door to be opened; but no servant went to open it. The knocks were repeated, if anything louder than before, the door swung back on its hinges, and the tread of heavy footsteps were heard slowly approaching the drawing-room. Mrs. Whittingen gave a low gasp of horror, Ruth screamed, Harvey buried his face in his hands, Mr. Whittingen rose to his feet, and made desperate efforts to get to the bell, but could not stir, whilst Martha rushed to the drawing-room door and locked it. They then with one accord began to pray. The steps halted outside the room, the door slowly opened, and the blurred outlines of a group of ghastly-looking figures, supporting a grotesquely shaped object in their midst, appeared on the threshold. For some seconds there was a grim silence. It was abruptly broken by a thud--Ruth had slipped from her chair to the floor in a dead faint; whereupon the shadowy forms solemnly veered round and made their way back again to the front door. The latter swung violently open, there was a rush of icy wind which swept like a hurricane across the hall and into the drawing-room, the front door then slammed to with a crash, and the coach drove away.

Every one's attention was now directed to Ruth. At first sal-volatile and cold water produced no effect, but after a time she slowly, very slowly regained consciousness. As soon as she had recovered sufficiently to speak, she expressed an earnest desire that no reference should ever be made in her presence to what had just happened. "It was for me!" she said in such an emphatic tone as filled her audience with the direst forebodings. "I know it was for me; they all looked in my direction. God help me! I shall die like Mary."

Though greatly perplexed as to what she meant, for no one excepting herself had been able to make out the phenomena with any degree of distinctness, they yielded to her entreaties, and asked her no questions. The servants had neither heard nor seen anything. A fortnight later, Ruth was taken ill with appendicitis; peritonitis speedily set in, and she died under the operation. The Whittingens now began to wish they had never come to Donaldgowerie; but, with the astuteness that had been characteristic of the family through countless generations of fair days and foul, they took the greatest precautions never to drop even as much as a hint to the servants or to any one in the town that the house was haunted.

A year passed without any further catastrophe, and they were beginning to hope their ghastly visitors had left them, when something else occurred. It was Easter-time, and Ernest, his wife, and baby were staying with them. The baby, a boy, was fat and bonny, the very picture of health and happiness.

Mrs. Whittingen and Martha vied with one another in their devotion to him; and either one or other of them was always dancing attendance on him. It so happened that one afternoon, whilst the servants were having their tea, Martha found herself alone in the upper part of the house with her precious nephew. Mr. Whittingen had gone to Edinburgh to consult his lawyer (the head of the firm with whom Harvey was articled) on business, whilst Mrs. Whittingen had taken her son and daughter-in-law for a drive. The weather was glorious, and Martha, though as little appreciative of the beauties of nature as most commercial-minded young women, could not but admire the colouring of the sky as she looked out of the nursery window. The sun had disappeared, but the effect of its rays was still apparent on the western horizon, where the heavens were washed with alternate streaks of gold and red and pink--the colour of each streak excessively brilliant in the centre, but paling towards the edges. Here and there were golden,

pink-tipped clouds and crimson islets surrounded
with seas of softest blue. And outside the limits of this
sun-kissed pale, the blue of the sky gradually grew
darker and darker, until its line was altogether lost in
the black shadows of night that, creeping over the lone
mountain-tops in the far east, slowly swept forward.
Wafted by the gentle breeze came the dull moaning
and whispering of the pine trees, the humming of the
wind through the telephone wires, and the discordant
cawing of the crows. And it seemed to Martha, as she
sat there and peered out into the garden, that over the
whole atmosphere of the place had come a subtle and
hostile change--a change in the noises of the trees, the
birds, the wind; a change in the flower-scented ether;
a change, a most marked and emphatic change, in the
shadows. What was it? What was this change?
Whence did it originate? What did it portend? A slight
noise, a most trivial noise, attracted Martha's
attention to the room; she looked round and was quite
startled to see how dark it had grown. In the old days,
when she had scoffed at ghosts, she would as soon
have been in the dark as in the light, the night had no
terrors for her; but now--now since those awful
occurrences last year, all was different, and as she
peered apprehensively about her, her flesh crawled.
What was there in that corner opposite, that corner
hemmed in on the one side by the cupboard--how she
hated cupboards, particularly when they had shiny
surfaces on which were reflected all sorts of curious
things--and the chest of drawers on the other. It was a
shadow, only a shadow, but of what? She searched the
room everywhere to find its material counterpart, and

at last discovered it in the nurse's shawl which hung over the back of a chair. Then she laughed, and would have gone on laughing, for she tried to persuade herself that laughter banished ghosts, when suddenly something else caught her eyes. What was it? An object that glittered evilly like two eyes. She got up in a state of the most hideous fascination and walked towards it. Then she laughed again--it was a pair of scissors. The nurse's scissors--clean, bright, and sharp. Why did she pick them up and feel the blades so caressingly with her thumb? Why did she glance from them to the baby? Why? In the name of God, why? Frightful ideas laid hold of her mind. She tried to chase them away but they quickly returned. The scissors, why were they in her fingers? Why could not she put them down? For what were they intended? Cutting! cutting thread, and tape,--and throats! Throats! And she giggled hysterically at the bare notion. But what was this round her waist--this shadowy arm-like object! She looked fearfully round, and her soul died within her as she encountered the malevolent, gleeful eyes of the sinister piper, pressed closely against her face. Was it she he wanted this time--she, or--or whom--in the name of all that was pitiable?

Desperately, as if all the lives in the universe and the future of her soul were at stake, did she struggle to free herself from his grasp--but in vain; every fibre, every muscle of her body was completely at his will. On and on he pushed her, until foot by foot, inch by inch, she approached the cradle, and all the while his hellish voice was breathing the vilest of inspirations into her brain. At last she stood by the side of the baby, and bent over it. What a darling! What a dear! What a duck! A sweet, pretty, innocent, prattling duck! How like her mother--how like her handsome brother--how like herself--very, very like herself! How every one loved it--how every one worshipped it--how (and here the grey face beside her chuckled) every one would miss it! How pink its toes--how fat its calves-- how chubby its little palms--how bonny its cheeks-- and how white, how gloriously, heavenly, snowy white--its throat! And she stretched forth one of her stubby, inartistic fingers and played with its flesh. Then she glanced furtively at the scissors, and smiled.

It was soon done, soon over, and she and the grey-faced piper danced a minuet in the moonbeams; afterwards he piped a farewell dirge,--a wild, weird, funereal dirge, and, marching slowly backwards, his dark, gleaming eyes fixed gloatingly on hers, disappeared through the window. Then the reaction set in, and Martha raved and shrieked till every one in the house flew to the rescue.

Of course, no one--saving her father and mother-- believed her. Ernest, his wife, and the servants attributed her bloody act to jealousy; the law--to madness; and she subsequently journeyed from Donaldgowerie to a criminal lunatic asylum, where the recollection of all she had done soon killed her. This was the climax. Mr. Whittingen sold

Donaldgowerie, and a new house was shortly afterwards erected in its stead.

CASE XIII

THE FLOATING HEAD OF THE BENRACHETT INN, NEAR THE PERTH ROAD, DUNDEE

Some years ago, when I was engaged in collecting cases for a book I contemplated publishing, on _Haunted Houses in England and Wales_, I was introduced to an Irish clergyman, whose name I have forgotten, and whom I have never met since. Had the incident he related taken place in England or Wales, I should have noted it down carefully, but as it occurred in Scotland (and I had no intention then of bringing out a volume on Scottish phantasms), I did not do so.

My memory, however, I can assure my readers, in spite of the many ghost tales committed to it,--for scarcely a day passes that I do not hear one,--seldom fails, and the Irish clergyman's story, which I am about to relate, comes back to me now with startling vividness.

One summer evening, early in the eighties, Mr. Murphy--the name by which I will designate the originator of this story--and his wife arrived in Dundee. The town was utterly unknown to them, and they were touring Scotland for the first time. Not knowing where to put up for the night, and knowing no one to whom they could apply for information, they consulted a local paper, and from the long list of hotels and boarding-houses advertised therein selected the Benrachett Inn, near the Perth Road, as being the one most likely to meet their modest requirements. They were certainly not disappointed with the exterior of the hotel they had chosen, for as soon as they saw it they exclaimed simultaneously, "What a delightful old place!" And old it certainly was, for the many-gabled, oaken structure and projecting windows unquestionably indicated the sixteenth century, whilst, to enhance the effect and give it a true touch in detail of "ye ancient times," a huge antique lantern was hung over the entrance. Nor did the interior impress them less favourably. The rooms were large, and low, the ceilings, walls, floors, and staircase all of oak. The diamond-lattice windows, and narrow, tortuous passages, and innumerable nooks and crannies and cupboards, created an atmosphere of combined quaintness and comfort that irresistibly appealed to the Murphys. Viewed under the searching rays of the sun, and cheered by the voices of the visitors, the interior of the house, for artistic taste and cheerfulness, would indeed be hard to beat; but, as Mrs. Murphy's eyes wandered up the stairs and down the corridors, she was filled with misgivings as to how the place would strike her at night.

Though not nervous naturally, and by no means superstitious, at night, when the house was dark and silent, and the moon called forth the shadows, she was not without that feeling of uneasiness which most people--even avowed sceptics, experience when passing the night in strange and novel quarters.

The room they engaged--I cannot say selected, as, the hotel being full, they had "Hobson's choice"--was at the end of a very long passage, at the back of the house, and overlooking the yard. It was a large apartment, and in one of its several recesses stood the bed, a gigantic, ebony four-poster, with spotlessly clean valance, and, what was of even greater importance, well-aired sheets. The other furniture in the room, being of the same sort as that in the majority of old-fashioned hostels, needs no description; but a fixture in the shape of a cupboard, a deep, dark cupboard, let into the wall facing the bed, instantly attracted Mrs. Murphy's attention. There is always something interesting in cupboards, particularly old and roomy cupboards, when it is night-time and one is about to get into bed. It is then that they suggest all manner of fascinating possibilities.

It was to this cupboard, then, that Mrs. Murphy paid the greatest attention, before commencing to undress prior to getting into bed. She poked about in it for some moments, and then, apparently satisfied that no one was hidden there, continued her investigation of the room. Mr. Murphy did not assist--he pleaded fatigue, and sat on the corner of the bed munching a gingerbread and reading the _Dundee Advertiser_ till the operation was over. He then helped Mrs. Murphy unpack their portmanteau, and, during the process, whiled away so much time in conversation, that they were both startled when a clock from some adjacent church solemnly boomed twelve. They were then seized with something approaching a panic, and hastened to disrobe.

"I wish we had a night-light, John," Mrs. Murphy said, as she got up from her prayers. "I suppose it wouldn't do to keep one of the candles burning. I am not exactly afraid, only I don't fancy being left in the dark. I had a curious sensation when I was in the cupboard just now--I can't exactly explain it--but I feel now that I would like the light left burning."

"It certainly is rather a gloomy room," Mr. Murphy remarked, raising his eyes to the black oak ceiling, and then allowing them to dwell in turn on each of the angles and recesses. "And I agree with you it would be nice if we had a night-light, or, better still, gas. But as we haven't, my dear, and we shall be on our feet a good deal to-morrow, I think we ought to try and get to sleep as soon as possible."

He blew out the candle as he spoke, and quickly scrambled into bed. A long hush followed, broken only by the sound of breathing, and an occasional ticking as of some long-legged creature on the wall and window-blind. Mrs. Murphy could never remember if she actually went to sleep, but she is sure her husband did, as she distinctly heard him snore-- and the sound, so detestable to her as a rule, was so welcome to her then. She was lying listening to it, and wishing with all her soul she could get to sleep, when she suddenly became aware of a smell--a most offensive, pungent odour, that blew across the room and crept up her nostrils. The cold perspiration of fear at once broke out on her forehead. Nasty as the smell was, it suggested something more horrible, something she dared not attempt to analyse. She thought several times of rousing her husband, but, remembering how tired he had been, she desisted, and, with all her faculties abnormally on the alert, she lay awake and listened. A deathlike hush hung over the house, interrupted at intervals by the surreptitious noises peculiar to the night--enigmatical creaks and footsteps, rustlings as of drapery, sighs and whisperings--all very faint, all very subtle, and all possibly, just possibly, attributable to natural causes. Mrs. Murphy caught herself--why, she could not say-- waiting for some definite auditory manifestation of what she instinctively felt was near at hand. At present, however, she could not locate it, she could only speculate on its whereabouts--it was somewhere in the direction of the cupboard. And each time the stench came to her, the conviction that its origin was in the cupboard grew. At last, unable to sustain the suspense any longer, and urged on by an irresistible fascination, she got softly out of bed, and, creeping stealthily forward, found her way with surprisingly little difficulty (considering it was pitch dark and the room was unfamiliar to her) to the cupboard.

With every step she took the stink increased, and by the time she had reached the cupboard she was almost suffocated. For some seconds she toyed irresolutely with the door handle, longing to be back again in bed, but unable to tear herself away from the cupboard. At last, yielding to the demands of some pitilessly exacting unknown influence, she held her breath and swung open the door. The moment she did so the room filled with the faint, phosphorescent glow of decay, and she saw, exactly opposite her, a head--a human head--floating in mid-air. Petrified with terror, she lost every atom of strength, and, entirely bereft of the power to move or articulate a sound, she stood stock-still staring at it. That it was the head of a man, she could only guess from the matted crop of short red hair that fell in a disordered entanglement over the upper part of the forehead and ears. All else was lost in a loathsome, disgusting mass of detestable decomposition, too utterly vile and foul to describe. On the abnormal thing beginning to move forward, the spell that bound Mrs. Murphy to the floor was broken, and, with a cry of horror, she fled to the bed and awoke her husband.

The head was by this time close to them, and had not Mrs. Murphy dragged her husband forcibly out of its way, it would have touched him.

His terror was even greater than hers; but for the moment neither could speak. They stood clutching one another in an awful silence. Mrs. Murphy at length gasped out, "Pray, John, pray! Command the thing in the name of God to depart." Mr. Murphy made a desperate effort to do so, but not a syllable would come. The head now veered round and was moving swiftly towards them, its awful stench causing them both to retch and vomit. Mr. Murphy, seizing his stick, lashed at it with all his might. The result was one they might well have expected. The stick met with no resistance, and the head continued to advance. Both Mr. and Mrs. Murphy then made a frantic attempt to find the door, the head still pursuing them, and, tripping over something in their wild haste, fell together on the floor. There was now no hope, the head had caught them up; it hovered immediately above them, and, descending lower, lower, and lower, finally passed right through them, through the floor, and out of sight. It was long ere either of them could sufficiently recover to stir from the floor, and when they did move, it was only to totter to their bed, and to lie with the bedclothes well over their heads, quivering and quaking till the morning.

The hot morning sun dissipating their fears, they got up, and, hurrying downstairs, demanded an interview with their landlord. It was in vain the latter argued it was all a nightmare they showed the absurdity of such a theory by vehemently attesting they had both simultaneously experienced the phenomena. They were about to take their departure, when the landlord, retracting all he had said, offered them another room and any terms they liked, "if only they would stay and hold their tongues."

"I know every word of what you say is true," he said, in such submissive tones that the tender hearts of Mr. and Mrs. Murphy instantly relented, and they promised to remain. "But what am I to do? I cannot shut up a house which I have taken on a twenty years' lease, because one room in it is haunted--and, after all, there is only one visitor in twenty who is disturbed by the apparition. What is the history of the head? Why, it is said to be that of a pedlar who was murdered here over a hundred years ago. The body was hidden behind the wainscoting, and his head under the cupboard floor. The miscreants were never caught; they are supposed to have gone down in a ship that sailed from this port just about that time and was never heard of again."

This is the gist of the story the clergyman told me, and, believing it as I undoubtedly do to be true, there is every reason to suppose that the inn, to which I have, of course, given a fictitious name, if still in existence, is still haunted.

CASE XIV

THE HAUNTINGS OF "---- HOUSE," IN THE NEIGHBOURHOOD OF THE GREAT WESTERN ROAD, ABERDEEN

The following experience of a haunting is that of Mr. Scarfe, who told it me some few summers ago, expressing at the same time great eagerness to accompany me on some of my investigations.

I append it as nearly as possible in his own words:--

I was spending Easter, he began, with some friends of mine in Aberdeen, and, learning from them that there was a haunted house in the immediate vicinity of the Great Western Road, I begged them to try and get me permission to spend a night in it. As good luck would have it, the landlord happened to be a connection of theirs, and although at first rather reluctant to give me leave, lest by doing so he should create a precedent, and, consequently, be pestered to death by people whom he knew to be as anxious as I was to see the ghost, he eventually yielded; and, the following evening at 8 p.m., accompanied only by my dog, Scott, I entered the premises.

I cannot say I felt very comfortable when the door slammed behind me, and I found myself standing alone in a cold, dark passage out of which rose a gloomy staircase, suggestive of all sorts of uncanny possibilities. However, overcoming these nervous apprehensions as best I could, I began a thorough search of the premises, to make sure that no one was hiding there.

Descending first of all into the basement, I explored the kitchen, scullery, larder, and other domestic offices. The place fairly reeked with damp, but this was not to be wondered at, taking in consideration the fact, that the soil was clay, the floor of the very poorest quality of cement, cracked and broken in a dozen and one places, and that there had been no fires in any of the rooms for many months. Here and there in the darkest corners were clusters of ugly cockroaches, whilst more than one monstrous rat scampered away on my approach. My dog, or rather the dog that was lent me, and which went by the name of Scott, kept close at my heel, showing no very great enthusiasm in his mission, and giving even the rodents as wide a berth as possible.

I invariably trust to my psychic faculty (as you know, Mr. O'Donnell, some people are born with the faculty) to enable me to detect the presence of the superphysical. I generally feel the latter incorporated in some inexplicable manner in the ether, or see it inextricably interwoven with the shadows.

Here in the basement it was everywhere--the air was simply saturated with it, and, as the fading sunlight called shadow after shadow into existence, it confronted me enigmatically whichever way I turned.

I went upstairs, and the presence followed me. In one or two of the top bedrooms--more particularly in a tiny garret overlooking the back-yard--the Presence seemed inclined to hover. For some seconds I waited there, in order to see if there would be any further development; there being none--I obeyed the mandates of a sudden impulse and made my way once more to the basement. On arriving at the top of the kitchen stairs, Scott showed a decided disinclination to descend farther. Crouching down, he whined piteously, and when I attempted to grasp him by the collar, snarled in a most savage manner. Consequently, thinking it better to have no companion at all than one so unwilling, I descended without him.

The stairs terminated in a very dark and narrow passage, into which the doors of the kitchen, larder, store room, etc., opened respectively, and at the farther extremity of which was a doorway leading to the back-yard. The superphysical Presence seeming to be more pronounced in this passage than anywhere else, I decided to spend the night in it, and, selecting a spot opposite the entrance to the scullery, I constructed a seat out of two of the drawers of the kitchen dresser, by placing them, one on the other, bottom uppermost on the floor.

It was now half-past nine; the traffic in the street overhead was beginning to diminish--the rumbling of drays or heavy four-wheelers had almost ceased, whilst the jingling of hansoms and even the piercing hoot-hoot and loud birr-birr of motors was fast becoming less and less frequent. I put out my candle and waited; and, as I waited, the hush and gloom of the house deepened and intensified, until, by midnight, all round me was black and silent--black with a blackness that defies penetration, and silent with a silence that challenges only the rivalry of the grave. Occasionally I heard sounds--such, for example, as the creaking of a board, the flopping of a cockroach, and the growling of Scott--sounds which in the daytime would have been too trivial to attract attention, but which now assumed the most startling and exaggerated proportions. From time to time I felt my pulse and took my temperature to make sure that I was perfectly normal, whilst at one o'clock, the hour when human vitality begins to be on the wane, I ate some chicken and ham sandwiches, which I helped down with a single glass of oatmeal stout. So far, beyond my feeling that there was a superphysical something in the house, nothing had occurred. There had not been the slightest attempt at manifestation, and, as the minutes sped swiftly by I began to fear that, perhaps, after all the hauntings were only of a negative nature. As the clock struck two, however, Scott gave an extra savage snarl, and the next moment came racing downstairs. Darting along the passage and tearing towards me, he scrambled up the overturned drawers, and, burying his face in my lap, set up the most piteous whinings. A sensation of icy coldness, such as could not have been due to any physical cause, now surged through me; and, as I got out my pocket flashlight ready for emergencies, I heard an unmistakable rustling in the cellar opposite. At once my whole attention became riveted in the direction of this sound, and, as I sat gazing fixedly in front of me, the darkness was suddenly dissipated and the whole passage, from one end to the other, was illuminated by a phosphorescent glow; which glow I can best describe as bearing a close resemblance, in kind though not in degree, to the glow of a glow-worm. I then saw the scullery door slowly begin to open. A hideous fear seized me. What--what in the name of Heaven should I see? Transfixed with terror, unable to move or utter a sound, I crouched against the wall paralysed, helpless; whilst the door opened wider and wider.

At last, at last after an interval which to me was eternity, Something, an as yet indefinite shadowy Something, loomed in the background of the enlargening space. My suspense was now sublime, and I felt that another second or so of such tension would assuredly see me swoon.

The shadowy Something, however, quickly developed, and, in less time than it takes to write, it assumed the form of a woman--a middle-aged woman with a startlingly white face, straight nose, and curiously lined mouth, the two front upper teeth of which projected considerably and were very long. Her hair was black, her hands coarse, and red, and she was clad in the orthodox shabby print of a general servant in some middle-class family. The expression in her wide-open, glassy blue eyes as they glared into mine was one of such intense mental and physical agony that I felt every atom of blood in my veins congeal. Creeping stealthily forward, her gaze still on me, she emerged from the doorway, and motioning to me to follow, glided up the staircase. Up, up, we went, the cold, grey dawn greeting us on our way. Entering the garret to which I have already alluded, the phantasm noiselessly approached the hearth, and, pointing downward with a violent motion of the index finger of its right hand, suddenly vanished. A great feeling of relief now came over me, and, yielding to a reaction which was the inevitable consequence of such a severe nervous strain, I reeled against the window-sill and shook with laughter.

Equanimity at length reasserting itself, I carefully marked the spot on the floor, indicated by the apparition, and descending into the basement to fetch Scott, made hurried tracks to my friends' house, where I was allowed to sleep on till late in the day. I then returned to the haunted house with the landlord, and my friend, and, on raising the boarding in the garret, we discovered a stamped and addressed envelope.

As the result of our combined inquiries, we learned that a few years previously the house had been occupied by some tradespeople of the name of

Piblington, who, some six or seven months before they left the house, had had in their employment a servant named Anna Webb. This servant, the description of whose person corresponded in every way with the ghost I had seen, had been suspected of stealing a letter containing money, and had hanged herself in the cellar.

The letter, I gathered, with several others, had been given to Anna to post by Mrs. Piblington, and as no reply to the one containing money was received, Anna was closely questioned. Naturally nervous and highly strung, the inquisition confused her terribly, and her embarrassment being construed into guilt, she was threatened with prosecution. "As a proof of my innocence," she scribbled on a piece of paper, which was produced at the subsequent inquest, "I am going to hang myself. I never stole your letter, and can only suppose it was lost in the post."

The mere fact of the accused committing suicide would, in many people's opinion, point to guilt; and as the postal order was never traced, it was generally concluded that Anna had secreted it, and had been only waiting till inquiries ceased, and the affair was forgotten, to cash it. Of course, the letter I found was the missing one, and although apparently hidden with intent, the fact of its never having been opened seemed to suggest that Anna was innocent, and that the envelope had, by some extraordinary accident, fallen unnoticed by Anna through the crack between the boards. Anyhow, its discovery put an end to the disturbances and the apparition of the unfortunate suicide--whether guilty or innocent, and the Judgment Day can alone determine that--has never been seen since.

CASE XV

THE WHITE LADY OF ROWNAM AVENUE, NEAR STIRLING

Like most European countries, Scotland claims its share of phantasms in the form of "White Ladies." According to Mr. Ingram, in his _Haunted Houses and Family Legends_, the ruins of the mansion of Woodhouselee are haunted by a woman in white, presumably (though, personally, I think otherwise) the ghost of Lady Hamilton of Bothwellhaugh. This unfortunate lady, together with her baby, was--during the temporary absence of her husband--stripped naked and turned out of doors on a bitterly cold night, by a favourite of the Regent Murray. As a result of this inhuman conduct the child died, and its mother, with the corpse in her arms, was discovered in the morning raving mad. Another instance of this particular form of apparition is to be found in Sir Walter Scott's

"White Lady of Avenel," and there are endless others, both in reality and fiction.

Some years ago, when I was putting up at a friend's house in Edinburgh, I was introduced to a man who had had several experiences with ghosts, and had, therefore, been especially asked to meet me. After we had talked together for some time, he related the following adventure which had befallen him, in his childhood, in Rownam avenue (the seat of Sir E.C.), near Stirling:--

I was always a lover of nature, he began, and my earliest reminiscences are associated with solitary rambles through the fields, dells, and copses surrounding my home. I lived within a stone's-throw of the property of old Sir E.C., who has long gone to rest--God bless his soul! And I think it needs blessing, for if there was any truth in local gossip (and it is said, I think truly, that "There is never any smoke without fire") he had lived a very queer life. Indeed, he was held in such universal awe and abhorrence that we used to fly at his approach, and never spoke of him amongst ourselves saving in such terms as "Auld dour crab," or "The laird deil."

Rownam Manor House, where he lived, was a fine specimen of sixteenth-century architecture, and had it been called a castle would have merited the appellation far more than many of the buildings in Scotland that bear that name. It was approached by a long avenue of trees--gigantic elms, oaks, and beeches, that, uniting their branches overhead in summertime, formed an effectual barrier to the sun's rays. This avenue had an irresistible attraction for me. It literally swarmed with rabbits and squirrels, and many are the times I have trespassed there to watch them. I had a very secure hiding-place in the hollow of an old oak, where I have often been secreted while Sir E.C. and his keepers, without casting a glance in my direction, passed unsuspectingly by, vowing all sorts of vengeance against trespassers.

Of course, I had to be very careful how I got there, for the grounds were well patrolled, and Sir E.C. had sworn to prosecute anyone he caught walking in them without his permission. Had Sir E.C. caught me, I should, doubtless, have been treated with the utmost severity, since he and my father were the most bitter opponents politically, and for that reason, unreasonable though it be, never lost an opportunity of insulting one another. My father, a strong Radical, was opposed to all big landed proprietors, and consequently winked his eye at my trespassings; but I think nothing would really have pleased him better than to have seen me brought to book by Sir E.C., since in my defence he would have had an opportunity of appealing to the passions of the local people, who were all Radicals, and of incensing them still further against the principles of feudalism.

But to continue. I had often heard it rumoured in the village that Rownam avenue was haunted, and that the apparition was a lady in white, and no other than Sir E.C.'s wife, whose death at a very early age had been hastened, if not entirely accounted for, by her husband's harsh treatment. Whether Sir E.C. was really as black as he was painted I have never been able to ascertain; the intense animosity with which we all regarded him, made us believe anything ill of him, and we were quite ready to attribute all the alleged hauntings in the neighbourhood to his past misdeeds. I believe my family, with scarcely an exception, believed in ghosts; anyhow, the subject of ghosts was so often discussed in my hearing that I became possessed of an ungovernable curiosity to see one. If only "The White Lady" would appear in the daytime, I thought, I should have no difficulty in satisfying this curiosity, but unfortunately she did not appear till night--in fact, not until long after boys of my age had been ruthlessly ordered off to bed. I did not quite like the idea of stealing out of the house at dead of night and going alone to see the ghost, so I suggested to my schoolfellow that he should also break loose one night and accompany me to Rownam to see "The White Lady." It was, however, of no use. Much as he would have liked to have seen a ghost in broad daylight, it was quite another matter at night, to say nothing of running the risk of being caught trespassing by that inveterate enemy, Sir E.C. At length, finding that neither persuasion, bribery, nor taunts of cowardice had any effect on my schoolfellow, who could not decide which appearance would be the more appalling, for,--he assured me I should be certain to encounter either one or the other--the White Lady, or the Laird Deil,--I gave up all further effort to induce him to accompany me, and made up my mind to go to Rownam avenue alone.

Biding my opportunity, and waiting till my father was safely out of the way,--on a visit to Greenock, where some business transaction would oblige him to remain for some days,--I climbed out of my bedroom window, when I deemed the rest of the household to be sound asleep, scudded swiftly across the fields, and, making short work of the lofty wall that formed the southernmost boundary of the Rownam estates, quickly made my way to the avenue. It was an ideal Sunday night in August, and it seemed as if all nature participated in the Sabbath abstraction from noise and work. Hardly a sound broke the exquisite silence of the woods. At times, overcome with the delightful sensation of freedom, I paused, and, raising my eyes to the starry heavens, drank in huge draughts of the pure country air, tainted only with the sweet smell of newly mown hay, and the scent of summer flowers. I became intoxicated, delirious, and in transports of joy threw myself on the soft mossy ground, and, baring my throat and chest, bathed myself in the moonbeams' kisses. Then, picking myself slowly up, I performed the maddest capers, and, finally sobering down, continued my course. Every now and again fancying I detected the stealthy footsteps of a keeper, I hid behind a tree, where I remained till I was quite assured I had been mistaken, and that no one was about. How long I dallied I do not know, but it must have been fully one o'clock before I arrived at the outskirts of the avenue, and, advancing eagerly, ensconced myself in my favourite sanctuary, the hollow oak. All was hushed and motionless, and, as I gazed into the gloom, I became conscious, for the first time in my life, of a sensation of eeriness. The arched canopy of foliage overhead was strongly suggestive of a funeral pall; not a glimmer of moonlight penetrated through it; and all beneath seemed to me to be buried in the silence and blackness of the grave.

The loneliness got on my nerves; at first I grew afraid, only afraid, and then my fears turned into a panic, a wild, mad panic, consisting in the one desire to get where there were human beings--creatures I knew and understood. With this end in view I emerged from my retreat, and was preparing to fly through the wood, when, from afar off, there suddenly came the sound of a voice, the harsh, grating voice of a man. Convinced this time that I had been discovered by a keeper, I jumped back into the tree, and, swarming up the inside of the trunk, peeped cautiously out. What I saw nearly made me jump out of my skin. Advancing along the avenue was the thing I had always longed to see, and for which I had risked so much: the mysterious, far-famed "Lady in White,"--a ghost, an actual, _bona fide_ ghost! How every nerve in my body thrilled with excitement, and my heart thumped--till it seemed on the verge of bursting through my ribs! "The Lady in White!" Why, it would be the talk of the whole countryside! Some one had _really_--no hearsay evidence--seen the notorious apparition at last. How all my schoolfellows would envy me, and how bitterly they would chide themselves for being too cowardly to accompany me! I looked at her closely, and noticed that she was entirely luminous, emitting a strong phosphorescent glow like the glow of a glow-worm, saving that it was in a perpetual state of motion. She wore a quantity of white drapery swathed round her in a manner that perplexed me sorely, until I suddenly realised with a creeping of my flesh that it must be a winding-sheet, that burial accessary so often minutely described to me by the son of the village undertaker. Though interesting, I did not think it at all becoming, and would have preferred to see any other style of garment. Streaming over her neck and shoulders were thick masses of long, wavy, golden hair, which was ruffled, but only slightly ruffled, by the gentle summer breeze. Her face, though terrifying by reason of its unearthly pallor, was so beautiful, that, had not some restraining influence compelled me to remain in hiding, I would have descended from my perch to obtain a nearer view of it. Indeed, I only once caught a glimpse of her full face, for, with a persistence that was most annoying, she kept it turned from me; but in that brief second the lustre of her long, blue eyes won my very soul, and boy as I was I felt, like the hero in song, that I would, for my bonnie ghost, in very deed, "lay me doon and dee."

Her eyes are still firmly impressed on my memory; I shall never forget them, any more than I shall forget the dainty curves of her full red lips and the snowy whiteness of her perfect teeth. Nothing, I thought, either on earth or in heaven could have been half so lovely, and I was so enraptured that it was not until she was directly beneath me that I perceived she was not alone, that walking by her side, with one arm round her waist, his face and figure illuminated with the light from her body, was Sir E.C. But how changed! Gone were the deep black scowl, the savage tightening of the jaws, and the intensely disagreeable expression that had earned for him the nickname of "The laird deil," and in their stead I saw _love_-- nothing but blind, infatuated, soul-devouring _love_--love for which no words can find an adequate description.

Throwing discretion to the wind--for my excitement and curiosity had risen to the highest pitch--I now thrust more than half my body out of the hole in the trunk. The next instant, with a cry of dismay, I pitched head first on to the ground.

It would seem that boys, like cats, cannot in ordinary circumstances be killed, and, instead of breaking my neck, I merely suffered that most immaterial injury--immaterial, at least, in my case--a temporary disendowment of the senses. On regaining the few wits I could lay claim to, I fully expected to find myself in the hands of the irate laird, who would seize me by the scruff of the neck and belabour me to pieces. Consequently, too frightened to move, I lay absolutely still with my eyes shut. But as the minutes glided by and nothing happened, I picked myself up. All was quiet and pitch dark--not a vestige of the "Lady in White"--not a vestige of Sir E.C.

It did not take me very long to get out of the wood and home. I ran all the way, and as it was still early--far too early for any of the household to be astir, I crept up to my bedroom unobserved. But not to sleep, oh dear me, no! not to sleep, for the moment I blew the candle out and got into bed, reaction set in, and I suffered agonies of fear!

When I went to school in the morning, my equilibrium restored, and, bubbling over with excitement to tell the boys what had happened, I received another shock--before I could ejaculate a word of my experiences, I was told--told with a roar and shout that almost broke the drum of my ears, that "the auld laird deil" was dead! His body had been found stretched on the ground, a few feet from the hollow oak, in the avenue shortly after sunrise. He had died from syncope, so the doctor said, that had probably been caused by a shock--some severe mental shock.

I did not tell my companions of my night's adventure after all. My eagerness to do so had departed when I heard of "the auld laird's" death.

CASE XVI

THE GHOST OF THE HINDOO CHILD, OR THE HAUNTINGS OF THE WHITE DOVE HOTEL, NEAR ST. SWITHIN'S STREET, ABERDEEN

In the course of many years' investigation of haunted houses, I have naturally come in contact with numerous people who have had first-hand experiences with the Occult. Nurse Mackenzie is one of these people. I met her for the first time last year at the house of my old friend, Colonel Malcolmson, whose wife she was nursing.

For some days I was hardly aware she was in the house, the illness of her patient keeping her in constant seclusion, but when Mrs. Malcolmson grew better, I not infrequently saw her, taking a morning "constitutional" in the beautiful castle grounds. It was on one of these occasions that she favoured me with an account of her psychical adventure.

It happened, she began, shortly after I had finished my term as probationer at St. K.'s Hospital, Edinburgh. A letter was received at the hospital one morning with the urgent request that two nurses should be sent to a serious case near St. Swithin's Street. As the letter was signed by a well-known physician in the town, it received immediate attention, and Nurse Emmett and I were dispatched, as day and night nurses respectively, to the scene of action. My hours on duty were from 9 p.m. till 9 a.m. The house in which the patient was located was the White Dove Hotel, a thoroughly respectable and well-managed establishment. The proprietor knew nothing about the invalid, except that her name was Vining, and that she had, at one period of her career, been an actress. He had noticed that she had looked ill on her arrival the previous week. Two days after her arrival, she had complained of feeling very ill, and the doctor, who had been summoned to attend her, said that she was suffering from a very loathsome Oriental disease, which, fortunately is, in this country, rare. The hotel, though newly decorated and equipped throughout with every up-to-date convenience, was in reality very old. It was one of those delightfully roomy erections that seem built for eternity rather than time, and for comfort rather than economy of space. The interior, with its oak-panelled walls, polished oak floors, and low ceilings, traversed with ponderous oaken beams, also impressed me pleasantly, whilst a flight of broad, oak stairs, fenced with balustrades a foot thick, brought me to a seemingly interminable corridor, into which the door of Miss Vining's room opened. It was a low, wainscoted apartment, and its deep-set window, revealing the thickness of the wall, looked out upon a dismal yard littered with brooms and buckets. Opposite the foot of the bed--a modern French bedstead, by the bye, whose brass fittings and somewhat flimsy hangings were strangely incongruous with their venerable surroundings--was an ingle, containing the smouldering relics of what had doubtless been intended for a fire, but which needed considerable coaxing before it could be converted from a pretence to a reality. There was no exit save by the doorway I had entered, and no furniture save a couple of rush-bottomed chairs and a table strewn with an untidy medley of writing materials and medicine bottles.

A feeling of depression, contrasting strangely with the effect produced on me by the cheerfulness of the hotel in general, seized me directly I entered the room. Despite the brilliancy of the electric light and the new and gaudy bed-hangings, the air was full of gloom--a gloom which, for the very reason that it was unaccountable, was the more alarming. I felt it hanging around me like the undeveloped shadow of something singularly hideous and repulsive, and, on my approaching the sick woman, it seemed to thrust itself in my way and force me back.

Miss Vining was decidedly good-looking; she had the typically theatrical features--neatly moulded nose and chin, curly yellow hair, and big, dreamy blue eyes that especially appeal to a certain class of men; like most women, however, I prefer something more solid, both physically and intellectually--I cannot stand "the pretty, pretty." She was, of course, far too ill to converse, and, beyond a few desultory and spasmodic ejaculations, maintained a rigid silence. As there was no occasion for me to sit close beside her, I drew up a chair before the fire, placing myself in such a position as to command a full view of the bed. My first night passed undisturbed by any incident, and in the morning the condition of my patient showed a slight improvement. It was eight o'clock in the evening when I came on duty again, and, the weather having changed during the day, the whole room echoed and re-echoed with the howling of the wind, which was raging round the house with demoniacal fury.

I had been at my post for a little over two hours--and had just registered my patient's temperature, when, happening to look up from the book I was reading, I saw to my surprise that the chair beside the head of the bed was occupied by a child--a tiny girl. How she had come into the room without attracting my attention was certainly extraordinary, and I could only suppose that the shrieking of the wind down the wide chimney had deadened the sound of the door and her footsteps.

I was naturally, of course, very indignant that she had dared to come in without rapping, and, getting up from my seat I was preparing to address her and bid her go, when she lifted a wee white hand and motioned me back. I obeyed because I could not help myself--her action was accompanied by a peculiar,-- an unpleasantly peculiar, expression that held me spellbound; and without exactly knowing why, I stood staring at her, tongue-tied and trembling. As her face was turned towards the patient, and she wore, moreover, a very wide-brimmed hat, I could see nothing of her features; but from her graceful little figure and dainty limbs, I gathered that she was probably both beautiful and aristocratic. Her dress, though not perhaps of the richest quality, was certainly far from shoddy, and there was something in its style and make that suggested foreign nationality,-- Italy--or Spain--or South America--or even the Orient, the probability of the latter being strengthened by her pose, which was full of the serpent-like ease which is characteristic of the East. I was so taken up with watching her that I forgot all about my patient, until a prolonged sigh from the bed reminded me of her existence. With an effort I then advanced, and was about to approach the bed, when the child, without moving her head, motioned me back, and--again I was helpless. The vision I had obtained of the sick woman, brief though it was, filled me with alarm. She was tossing to and fro on the blankets, and breathing in the most agonised manner as if in delirium, or enthralled by some particularly dreadful nightmare. Her condition so frightened me, that I made the most frantic efforts to overcome my inertia. I did not succeed, however, and at last, utterly overcome by my exertion, I closed my eyes. When I opened them again, the chair by the bed was vacant--the child had gone. A tremendous feeling of relief surged through me, and, jumping out of my seat, I hastened to the bedside--my patient was worse, the fever had increased, and she was delirious. I took her temperature. It was 104. I now sat close beside her, and my presence apparently had a soothing effect. She speedily grew calmer, and after taking her medicine gradually sank into a gentle sleep which lasted until late in the morning. When I left her she had altogether recovered from the relapse. I, of course, told the doctor of the child's visit, and he was very angry.

"Whatever happens, Nurse," he said, "take care that no one enters the room to-night; the patient's condition is far too critical for her to see any one, even her own daughter. You must keep the door locked."

Armed with this mandate, I went on duty the following night with a somewhat lighter heart, and, after locking the door, once again sat by the fire. During the day there had been a heavy fall of snow; the wind had abated, and the streets were now as silent as the grave.

Ten, eleven, and twelve o'clock struck, and my patient slept tranquilly. At a quarter to one, however, I was abruptly roused from a reverie by a sob, a sob of fear and agony that proceeded from the bed. I looked, and there--there, seated in the same posture as on the previous evening, was the child. I sprang to my feet with an exclamation of amazement. She raised her hand, and, as before, I collapsed--spellbound-- paralysed. No words of mine can convey all the sensations I experienced as I sat there, forced to listen to the moaning and groaning of the woman whose fate had been entrusted to my keeping. Every second she grew worse, and each sound rang in my ears like the hammering of nails in her coffin. How long I endured such torment I cannot say, I dare not think, for, though the clock was within a few feet of me, I never once thought of looking at it. At last the child rose, and, moving slowly from the bed, advanced with bowed head towards the window. The spell was broken. With a cry of indignation I literally bounded over the carpet and faced the intruder.

"Who are you?" I hissed. "Tell me your name instantly! How dare you enter this room without my permission?"

As I spoke she slowly raised her head. I snatched at her hat. It melted away in my hands, and, to my unspeakable terror, my undying terror, I looked into the face of a corpse!--the corpse of a Hindoo child, with a big, gaping cut in its throat. In its lifetime the child had, without doubt, been lovely; it was now horrible--horrible with all the ghastly disfigurements, the repellent disfigurements, of a long consignment to the grave. I fainted, and, on recovering, found my ghostly visitor had vanished, and that my patient was dead. One of her hands was thrown across her eyes, as if to shut out some object on which she feared to look, whilst the other grasped the counterpane convulsively.

It fell to my duty to help pack up her belongings, and among her letters was a large envelope bearing the postmark "Quetta." As we were on the look-out for some clue as to the address of her relatives, I opened it. It was merely the cabinet-size photograph of a Hindoo child, but I recognised the dress immediately-

-it was that of my ghostly visitor. On the back of it were these words: "Natalie. May God forgive us both."

Though we made careful inquiries for any information as to Natalie and Miss Vining in Quetta, and advertised freely in the leading London papers, we learned nothing, and in time we were forced to let the matter drop. As far as I know, the ghost of the Hindoo child has never been seen again, but I have heard that the hotel is still haunted--haunted by a woman.

CASE XVII

GLAMIS CASTLE

Of all the hauntings in Scotland, none has gained such widespread notoriety as the hauntings of Glamis Castle, the seat of the Earl of Strathmore and Kinghorne in Forfarshire.

Part of the castle--that part which is the more frequently haunted--is of ancient though uncertain date, and if there is any truth in the tradition that Duncan was murdered there by Macbeth, must, at any rate, have been in existence at the commencement of the eleventh century. Of course, extra buildings have, from time to time, been added, and renovations made; but the original structure remains pretty nearly the same as it always has been, and is included in a square tower that occupies a central position, and commands a complete view of the entire castle.

Within this tower--the walls of which are fifteen feet thick--there is a room, hidden in some unsuspected quarter, that contains a secret (the keynote to one, at least, of the hauntings) which is known only to the Earl, his heir (on the attainment of his twenty-first birthday), and the factor of the estate.

In all probability, the mystery attached to this room would challenge but little attention, were it not for the fact that unearthly noises, which at the time were supposed to proceed from this chamber, have been heard by various visitors sleeping in the Square Tower.

The following experience is said to have happened to a lady named Bond. I append it more or less in her own words.

* * * * *

It is a good many years since I stayed at Glamis. I was, in fact, but little more than a child, and had only just gone through my first season in town. But though young, I was neither nervous nor imaginative; I was inclined to be what is termed stolid, that is to say, extremely matter-of-fact and practical. Indeed, when my friends exclaimed, "You don't mean to say you are going to stay at Glamis! Don't you know it's haunted?" I burst out laughing.

"Haunted!" I said, "how ridiculous! There are no such things as ghosts. One might as well believe in fairies."

Of course I did not go to Glamis alone--my mother and sister were with me; but whereas they slept in the more modern part of the castle, I was, at my own request, apportioned a room in the Square Tower.

I cannot say that my choice had anything to do with the secret chamber. That, and the alleged mystery, had been dinned into my ears so often that I had grown thoroughly sick of the whole thing. No, I wanted to sleep in the Square Tower for quite a different reason, a reason of my own. I kept an aviary; the tower was old; and I naturally hoped its walls would be covered with ivy and teeming with birds' nests, some of which I might be able to reach--and, I am ashamed to say, plunder--from my window.

Alas, for my expectations! Although the Square Tower was so ancient that in some places it was actually crumbling away--not the sign of a leaf, not the vestige of a bird's nest could I see anywhere; the walls were abominably, brutally bare. However, it was not long before my disappointment gave way to delight; for the air that blew in through the open window was so sweet, so richly scented with heather and honeysuckle, and the view of the broad, sweeping, thickly wooded grounds so indescribably charming, that, despite my inartistic and unpoetical nature, I was entranced--entranced as I had never been before, and never have been since. "Ghosts!" I said to myself, "ghosts! how absurd! how preposterously absurd! such an adorable spot as this can only harbour sunshine and flowers."

I well remember, too--for, as I have already said, I was not poetical--how much I enjoyed my first dinner at Glamis. The long journey and keen mountain air had made me hungry, and I thought I had never tasted such delicious food--such ideal salmon (from the Esk) and such heavenly fruit. But I must tell you that, although I ate heartily, as a healthy girl should, by the time I went to bed I had thoroughly digested my meal, and was, in fact, quite ready to partake of a few oatmeal biscuits I found in my dressing-case, and remembered having bought at Perth. It was about eleven o'clock when my maid left me, and I sat for some minutes wrapped in my dressing gown, before the open window. The night was very still, and save for an occasional rustle of the wind in the distant tree-tops, the hooting of an owl, the melancholy cry of a peewit and the hoarse barking of a dog, the silence was undisturbed.

The interior of my room was, in nearly every particular, modern. The furniture was not old; there were no grim carvings; no grotesquely-fashioned tapestries on the walls; no dark cupboards; no gloomy corners;--all was cosy and cheerful, and when I got into bed no thought of bogle or mystery entered my mind.

In a few minutes I was asleep, and for some time there was nothing but a blank--a blank in which all identity was annihilated. Then suddenly I found myself in an oddly-shaped room with a lofty ceiling, and a window situated at so great a distance from the black oaken floor as to be altogether inaccessible from within. Feeble gleams of phosphorescent light made their way through the narrow panes, and served to render distinct the more prominent objects around; but my eyes struggled in vain to reach the remoter angles of the wall, one of which inspired me with terror such as I had never felt before. The walls were covered with heavy draperies that were sufficient in themselves to preclude the possibility of any save the loudest of sounds penetrating without.

The furniture, if such one could call it, puzzled me. It seemed more fitted for the cell of a prison or lunatic asylum, or even for a kennel, than for an ordinary dwelling-room. I could see no chair, only a coarse deal table, a straw mattress, and a kind of trough. An air of irredeemable gloom and horror hung over and pervaded everything. As I stood there, I felt I was waiting for something--something that was concealed in the corner of the room I dreaded. I tried to reason with myself, to assure myself that there was nothing there that could hurt me, nothing that could even terrify me, but my efforts were in vain--my fears grew. Had I had some definite knowledge as to the cause of my alarm I should not have suffered so much, but it was my ignorance of what was there, of what I feared, that made my terror so poignant. Each second saw the agony of my suspense increase. I dared not move. I hardly dare breathe, and I dreaded lest the violent pulsation of my heart should attract the attention of the Unknown Presence and precipitate its coming out. Yet despite the perturbation of my mind, I caught myself analysing my feelings. It was not danger I abhorred so much, as its absolute effect--fright. I shuddered at the bare thought of what result the most trivial incident--the creaking of a board, ticking of a beetle, or hooting of an owl--might have on the intolerable agitation of my soul.

In this unnerved and pitiable condition I felt that the period was bound to come, sooner or later, when I should have to abandon life and reason together in the most desperate of struggles with--fear.

At length, something moved. An icy chill ran through my frame, and the horror of my anticipations immediately reached its culminating point. The Presence was about to reveal itself.

The gentle rubbing of a soft body on the floor, the crack of a bony joint, breathing, another crack, and then--was it my own excited imagination--or the disturbing influence of the atmosphere--or the uncertain twilight of the chamber that produced before me, in the stygian darkness of the recess, the vacillating and indistinct outline of something luminous, and horrid? I would gladly have risked futurity to have looked elsewhere--I could not. My eyes were fixed--I was compelled to gaze steadily in front of me.

Slowly, very slowly, the thing, whatever it was, took shape. Legs--crooked, misshapen, human legs. A body--tawny and hunched. Arms--long and spidery, with crooked, knotted fingers. A head--large and bestial, and covered with a tangled mass of grey hair that hung around its protruding forehead and pointed ears in ghastly mockery of curls. A face--and herein was the realisation of all my direst expectations--a face--white and staring, piglike in formation, malevolent in expression; a hellish combination of all things foul and animal, and yet withal not without a touch of pathos.

As I stared at it aghast, it reared itself on its haunches after the manner of an ape, and leered piteously at me. Then, shuffling forward, it rolled over, and lay sprawled out like some ungainly turtle--and wallowed, as for warmth, in the cold grey beams of early dawn.

At this juncture the handle of the chamber door turned, some one entered, there was a loud cry--and I awoke--awoke to find the whole tower, walls and rafters, ringing with the most appalling screams I have ever heard,--screams of some thing or of some one--for there was in them a strong element of what was human as well as animal--in the greatest distress.

Wondering what it meant, and more than ever terrified, I sat up in bed and listened,--listened whilst a conviction--the result of intuition, suggestion, or what you will, but a conviction all the same--forced me to associate the sounds with the thing in my dream. And I associate them still.

* * * * *

It was, I think, in the same year--in the year that the foregoing account was narrated to me--that I heard another story of the hauntings at Glamis, a story in connection with a lady whom I will call Miss Macginney. I append her experience as nearly as possible as she is stated to have told it.

* * * * *

I seldom talk about my adventure, Miss Maginney announced, because so many people ridicule the superphysical, and laugh at the mere mention of ghosts. I own I did the same myself till I stayed at Glamis; but a week there quite cured me of scepticism, and I came away a confirmed believer.

The incident occurred nearly twenty years ago--
shortly after my return from India, where my father
was then stationed.

It was years since I had been to Scotland, indeed I had
only once crossed the border and that when I was a
babe; consequently I was delighted to receive an
invitation to spend a few weeks in the land of my
birth. I went to Edinburgh first--I was born in
Drumsheugh Gardens--and thence to Glamis.

It was late in the autumn, the weather was intensely
cold, and I arrived at the castle in a blizzard. Indeed, I
do not recollect ever having been out in such a
frightful storm. It was as much as the horses could do
to make headway, and when we reached the castle we
found a crowd of anxious faces eagerly awaiting us in
the hall.

Chilled! I was chilled to the bone, and thought I never
should thaw. But the huge fires and bright and cosy
atmosphere of the rooms--for the interior of Glamis
was modernised throughout--soon set me right, and
by tea time I felt nicely warm and comfortable.

My bedroom was in the oldest part of the castle--the
Square Tower--but although I had been warned by
some of the guests that it might be haunted, I can
assure you that when I went to bed no subject was
farther from my thoughts than the subject of ghosts. I
returned to my room at about half-past eleven. The
storm was then at its height--all was babel and
confusion--impenetrable darkness mingled with the

wildest roaring and shrieking; and when I peeped through my casement window I could see nothing-- the panes were shrouded in snow--snow which was incessantly dashed against them with cyclonic fury. I fixed a comb in the window-frame so as not to be kept awake by the constant jarring; and with the caution characteristic of my sex looked into the wardrobe and under the bed for burglars--though Heaven knows what I should have done had I found one there-- placed a candlestick and matchbox on the table by my bedside, lest the roof or window should be blown in during the night or any other catastrophe happen, and after all these preparations got into bed. At this period of my life I was a sound sleeper, and, being somewhat unusually tired after my journey, I was soon in a dreamless slumber. What awoke me I cannot say, but I came to myself with a violent start, such as might have been occasioned by a loud noise. Indeed, that was, at first, my impression, and I strained my ears to try and ascertain the cause of it. All was, however, silent. The storm had abated, and the castle and grounds were wrapped in an almost preternatural hush. The sky had cleared, and the room was partially illuminated by a broad stream of silvery light that filtered softly in through the white and tightly drawn blinds. A feeling that there was something unnatural in the air, that the stillness was but the prelude to some strange and startling event, gradually came over me. I strove to reason with myself, to argue that the feeling was wholly due to the novelty of my surroundings, but my efforts were fruitless. And soon there stole upon me a sensation to which I had been hitherto an utter stranger--I became afraid. An irrepressible tremor pervaded my frame, my teeth chattered, my blood froze. Obeying an impulse--an impulse I could not resist, I lifted myself up from the pillows, and, peering fearfully into the shadowy glow that lay directly in front of me--listened. Why I listened I do not know, saving that an instinctive spirit prompted me. At first I could hear nothing, and then, from a direction I could not define, there came a noise, low, distinct, uninterpretative. It was repeated in rapid succession, and speedily construed itself into the sound of mailed footsteps racing up the long flight of stairs at the end of the corridor leading to my room. Dreading to think what it might be, and seized with a wild sentiment of self-preservation, I made frantic endeavours to get out of bed and barricade my door. My limbs, however, refused to move. I was paralysed. Nearer and nearer drew the sounds; and I could at length distinguish, with a clearness that petrified my very soul, the banging and clanging of sword scabbards, and the panting and gasping of men, sore pressed in a wild and desperate race. And then the meaning of it all came to me with hideous abruptness--it was a case of pursued and pursuing--the race was for--LIFE. Outside my door the fugitive halted, and from the noise he made in trying to draw his breath, I knew he was dead beat. His antagonist, however, gave him but scant time for recovery. Bounding at him with prodigious leaps, he struck him a blow that sent him reeling with such tremendous force against the door, that the panels, although composed of the stoutest oak, quivered and strained like flimsy matchboard.

173

The blow was repeated; the cry that rose in the victim's throat was converted into an abortive gurgling groan; and I heard the ponderous battle-axe carve its way through helmet, bone, and brain. A moment later came the sound of slithering armour; and the corpse, slipping sideways, toppled to the ground with a sonorous clang.

A silence too awful for words now ensued. Having finished his hideous handiwork, the murderer was quietly deliberating what to do next; whilst my dread of attracting his attention was so great that I scarcely dare breathe. This intolerable state of things had already lasted for what seemed to me a lifetime, when, glancing involuntarily at the floor, I saw a stream of dark-looking fluid lazily lapping its way to me from the direction of the door. Another moment and it would reach my shoes. In my dismay I shrieked aloud. There was a sudden stir without, a significant clatter of steel, and the next moment--despite the fact that it was locked--the door slowly opened. The limits of my endurance had now happily been reached, the over-taxed valves of my heart could stand no more--I fainted. On my awakening to consciousness it was morning, and the welcome sun rays revealed no evidences of the distressing drama. I own I had a hard tussle before I could make up my mind to spend another night in that room; and my feelings as I shut the door on my retreating maid, and prepared to get into bed, were not the most enviable. But nothing happened, nor did I again experience anything of the sort till the evening before I left. I had lain down all the afternoon--for I was tired after a long morning's tramp on the moors, a thing I dearly love--and I was thinking it was about time to get up, when a dark shadow suddenly fell across my face.

I looked up hastily, and there, standing by my bedside and bending over me, was a gigantic figure in bright armour.

Its visor was up, and what I saw within the casque is stamped for ever on my memory. It was the face of the dead--the long since dead--with the expression--the subtly hellish expression--of the living. As I gazed helplessly at it, it bent lower. I threw up my hands to ward it off. There was a loud rap at the door. And as my maid softly entered to tell me tea was ready--it vanished.

* * * * *

The third account of the Glamis hauntings was told me as long ago as the summer of 1893. I was travelling by rail from Perth to Glasgow, and the only other occupant of my compartment was an elderly gentleman, who, from his general air and appearance, might have been a dominie, or member of some other learned profession. I can see him in my mind's eye now--a tall, thin man with a premature stoop. He had white hair, which was brushed forward on either side of his head in such a manner as suggested a wig;

bushy eyebrows; dark, piercing eyes; and a stern, though somewhat sad, mouth. His features were fine and scholarly; he was clean-shaven. There was something about him--something that marked him from the general horde--something that attracted me, and I began chatting with him soon after we left Perth.

In the course of a conversation, that was at all events interesting to me, I adroitly managed to introduce the subject of ghosts--then, as ever, uppermost in my thoughts.

* * * * *

Well, he said, I can tell you of something rather extraordinary that my mother used to say happened to a friend of hers at Glamis. I have no doubt you are well acquainted with the hackneyed stories in connection with the hauntings at the castle; for example, Earl Beardie playing cards with the Devil, and The Weeping Woman without Hands or Tongue. You can read about them in scores of books and magazines. But what befel my mother's friend, whom I will call Mrs. Gibbons--for I have forgotten her proper name--was apparently of a novel nature. The affair happened shortly before Mrs. Gibbons died, and I always thought that what took place might have been, in some way, connected with her death.

She had driven over to the castle one day--during the absence of the owner--to see her cousin, who was in the employ of the Earl and Countess. Never having been at Glamis before, but having heard so much about it, Mrs. Gibbons was not a little curious to see that part of the building, called the Square Tower, that bore the reputation of being haunted.

Tactfully biding an opportunity, she sounded her relative on the subject, and was laughingly informed that she might go anywhere about the place she pleased, saving to one spot, namely, "Bluebeard's Chamber"; and there she could certainly never succeed in poking her nose, as its locality was known only to three people, all of whom were pledged never to reveal it. At the commencement of her tour of inspection, Mrs. Gibbons was disappointed--she was disappointed in the Tower. She had expected to see a gaunt, grim place, crumbling to pieces with age, full of blood-curdling, spiral staircases, and deep, dark dungeons; whereas everything was the reverse. The walls were in an excellent state of preservation-- absolutely intact; the rooms bright and cheerful and equipped in the most modern style; there were no dungeons, at least none on view, and the passages and staircases were suggestive of nothing more alarming than--bats! She was accompanied for some time by her relative, but, on the latter being called away, Mrs. Gibbons continued her rambles alone. She had explored the lower premises, and was leisurely examining a handsomely furnished apartment on the top floor, when, in crossing from one side of the room to the other, she ran into something. She looked down--nothing was to be seen. Amazed beyond description, she thrust out her hands, and they alighted on an object, which she had little difficulty in identifying. It was an enormous cask or barrel lying in a horizontal position.

She bent down close to where she felt it, but she could see nothing--nothing but the well-polished boards of the floor. To make sure again that the barrel was there, she gave a little kick--and drew back her foot with a cry of pain. She was not afraid--the sunshine in the room forbade fear--only exasperated. She was certain a barrel was there--that it was objective--and she was angry with herself for not seeing it. She wondered if she were going blind; but the fact that other objects in the room were plainly visible to her, discountenanced such an idea. For some minutes she poked and jabbed at the Thing, and then, seized with a sudden and uncontrollable panic, she turned round and fled. And as she tore out of the room, along the passage and down the seemingly interminable flight of stairs, she heard the barrel behind her in close pursuit-bump--bump--bump!

At the foot of the staircase Mrs. Gibbons met her cousin, and, as she clutched the latter for support, the barrel shot past her, still continuing its descent--bump--bump--bump! (though the steps as far as she could see had ended)--till the sounds gradually dwindled away in the far distance.

Whilst the manifestations lasted, neither Mrs. Gibbons nor her cousin spoke; but the latter, as soon as the sounds had ceased, dragged Mrs. Gibbons away, and, in a voice shaking with terror, cried:

"Quick, quick--don't, for Heaven's sake, look round--worse has yet to come." And, pulling Mrs. Gibbons along in breathless haste, she unceremoniously hustled her out of the Tower.

"That was no barrel!" Mrs. Gibbons's cousin subsequently remarked by way of explanation. "I saw it--I have seen it before. Don't ask me to describe it. I dare not--I dare not even think of it. Whenever it appears, a certain thing happens shortly afterwards. Don't, don't on any account say a word about it to any one here." And Mrs. Gibbons, my mother told me, came away from Glamis a thousand times more curious than she was when she went.

* * * * *

The last story I have to relate is one I heard many years ago, when I was staying near Balmoral. A gentleman named Vance, with strong antiquarian tastes, was staying at an inn near the Strathmore estate, and, roaming abroad one afternoon, in a fit of absent-mindedness entered the castle grounds. It so happened--fortunately for him--that the family were away, and he encountered no one more formidable than a man he took to be a gardener, an uncouth-looking fellow, with a huge head covered with a mass of red hair, hawk-like features, and high cheek-bones, high even for a Scot. Struck with the appearance of the individual, Mr. Vance spoke, and, finding him wonderfully civil, asked whether, by any chance, he ever came across any fossils, when digging in the gardens.

"I dinna ken the meaning of fossils," the man replied. "What are they?"

Mr. Vance explained, and a look of cunning gradually pervaded the fellow's features. "No!" he said, "I've never found any of those things, but if you'll give me your word to say nothing about it, I'll show you something I once dug up over yonder by the Square Tower."

"Do you mean the Haunted Tower?--the Tower that is supposed to contain the secret room?" Mr. Vance exclaimed.

An extraordinary expression--an expression such as Mr. Vance found it impossible to analyse--came into the man's eyes. "Yes! that's it!" he nodded. "What people call--and rightly call--the Haunted Tower. I got it from there. But don't you say naught about it!"

Mr. Vance, whose curiosity was roused, promised, and the man, politely requesting him to follow, led the way to a cottage that stood near by, in the heart of a gloomy wood. To Mr. Vance's astonishment the treasure proved to be the skeleton of a hand--a hand with abnormally large knuckles, and the first joint--of both fingers and thumb--much shorter than the others. It was the most extraordinarily shaped hand

Mr. Vance had ever seen, and he did not know in the least how to classify it. It repelled, yet interested him, and he eventually offered the man a good sum to allow him to keep it. To his astonishment the money was refused. "You may have the thing, and welcome," the fellow said. "Only, I advise you not to look at it late at night; or just before getting into bed. If you do, you may have bad dreams."

"I will take my chance of that!" Mr. Vance laughed. "You see, being a hard-headed cockney, I am not superstitious. It is only you Highlanders, and your first cousins the Irish, who believe nowadays in bogles, omens, and such-like"; and, packing the hand carefully in his knapsack, Mr. Vance bid the strange-looking creature good morning, and went on his way.

For the rest of the day the hand was uppermost in his thoughts--nothing had ever fascinated him so much. He sat pondering over it the whole evening, and bedtime found him still examining it--examining it upstairs in his room by candlelight. He had a hazy recollection that some clock had struck twelve, and he was beginning to feel that it was about time to retire, when, in the mirror opposite him, he caught sight of the door--it was open.

"By Jove! that's odd!" he said to himself. "I could have sworn I shut and bolted it." To make sure, he turned round--the door was closed. "An optical delusion," he murmured; "I will try again."

He looked into the mirror--the door reflected in it was--open. Utterly at a loss to know how to explain the phenomenon, he leaned forward in his seat to examine the glass more carefully, and as he did so he gave a start. On the threshold of the doorway was a shadow--black and bulbous. A cold shiver ran down Mr. Vance's spine, and just for a moment he felt afraid, terribly afraid; but he quickly composed himself--it was nothing but an illusion--there was no shadow there in reality--he had only to turn round, and the thing would be gone. It was amusing-- entertaining. He would wait and see what happened.

The shadow moved. It moved slowly through the air like some huge spider, or odd-shaped bird. He would not acknowledge that there was anything sinister about it--only something droll--excruciatingly droll. Yet it did not make him laugh. When it had drawn a little nearer, he tried to diagnose it, to discover its material counterpart in one of the objects around him; but he was obliged to acknowledge his attempts were failures--there was nothing in the room in the least degree like it. A vague feeling of uneasiness gradually crept over him--was the thing the shadow of something with which he was familiar, but could not just then recall to mind--something he feared-- something that was sinister? He struggled against the idea, he dismissed it as absurd; but it returned-- returned, and took deeper root as the shadow drew nearer. He wished the house was not quite so silent-- that he could hear some indication of life--anything-- anything for companionship, and to rid him of the oppressive, the very oppressive, sense of loneliness and isolation.

Again a thrill of terror ran through him.

"Look here!" he exclaimed aloud, glad to hear the sound of his own voice. "Look here! if this goes on much longer I shall begin to think I'm going mad. I have had enough, and more than enough, of magic mirrors for one night--it's high time I got into bed." He strove to rise from his chair--to move; he was unable to do either; some strange, tyrannical force held him a prisoner.

A change now took place in the shadow; the blurr dissipated, and the clearly defined outlines of an object--an object that made Mr. Vance perfectly sick with apprehension--slowly disclosed themselves. His suspicions were verified--it was the HAND!--the hand--no longer skeleton, but covered with green, mouldering flesh--feeling its way slyly and stealthily towards him--towards the back of his chair! He noted the murderous twitching of its short, flat finger-tips, the monstrous muscles of its hideous thumb, and the great, clumsy hollows of its clammy palm. It closed in upon him; its cold, slimy, detestable skin touched his coat--his shoulder--his neck--his head! It pressed him down, squashed, suffocated him! He saw it all in the glass--and then an extraordinary thing happened. Mr. Vance suddenly became animated. He got up and peeped furtively round. Chairs, bed, wardrobe, had all disappeared--so had the bedroom--and he found himself in a small, bare, comfortless, queerly

constructed apartment without a door, and with only
a narrow slit of a window somewhere near the ceiling.

He had in one of his hands a knife with a long, keen
blade, and his whole mind was bent on murder.
Creeping stealthily forward, he approached a corner
of the room, where he now saw, for the first time--a
mattress--a mattress on which lay a huddled-up form.
What the Thing was--whether human or animal--Mr.
Vance did not know--did not care--all he felt was that
it was there for him to kill--that he loathed and hated
it--hated it with a hatred such as nothing else could
have produced. Tiptoeing gently up to it, he bent
down, and, lifting his knife high above his head,
plunged it into the Thing's body with all the force he
could command.

* * * * *

He recrossed the room, and found himself once more
in his apartment at the inn. He looked for the skeleton
hand--it was not where he had left it--it had vanished.
Then he glanced at the mirror, and on its brilliantly
polished surface saw--not his own face--but the face of
the gardener, the man who had given him the hand!
Features, colour, hair--all--all were identical--
wonderfully, hideously identical--and as the eyes met
his, they smiled--devilishly.

* * * * *

Early the next day, Mr. Vance set out for the spinney and cottage; they were not to be found--nobody had ever heard of them. He continued his travels, and some months later, at a loan collection of pictures in a gallery in Edinburgh, he came to an abrupt--a very abrupt--halt, before the portrait of a gentleman in ancient costume. The face seemed strangely familiar-- the huge head with thick, red hair--the hawk-like features--the thin and tightly compressed lips. Then, in a trice, it all came back to him: the face he looked at was that of the uncouth gardener--the man who had given him the hand. And to clinch the matter, the eyes--leered.